Mein
PROJEKT

NOTIZBUCH FÜR
OLDTIMERSCHRAUBER

Steffi Kopf

Mein
PROJEKT

NOTIZBUCH FÜR OLDTMERSCHRAUBER

Praktischer Werkstattbegleiter für alle, die ihr
historisches Blech selbst warten

RED RAVEN
BusinessBooks

Bibliografische Information der Deutschen Nationalbibliothek:
Die Deutsche Nationalbibliothek verzeichnet diese Publikation in der Deutschen Nationalbibliografie; detaillierte bibliografische Daten sind im Internet über http://dnb.dnb.de abrufbar.

Herstellung und Verlag: BoD – Books on Demand, Norderstedt
ISBN: 978-3-750423077

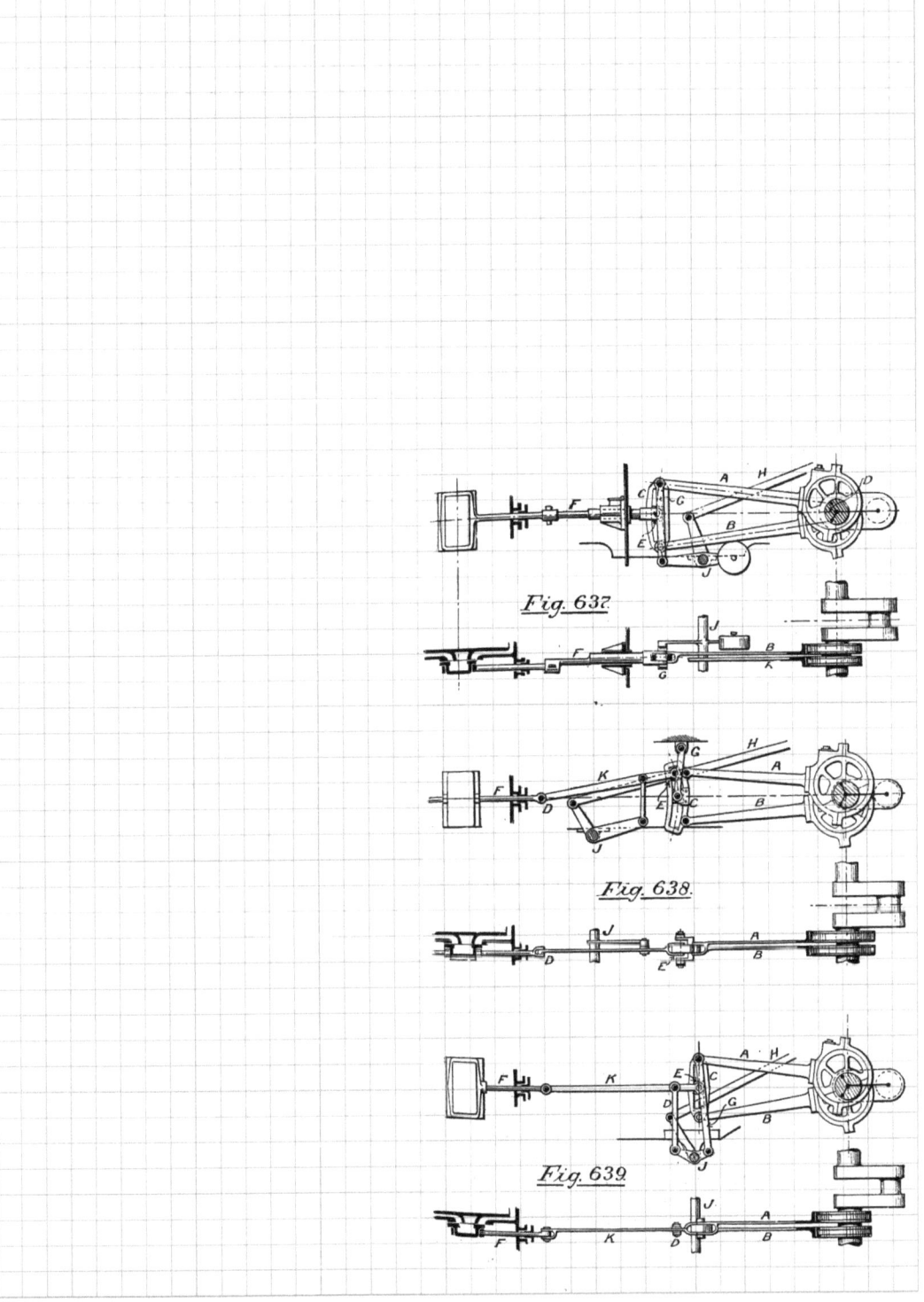

Fig. 637

Fig. 638

Fig. 639

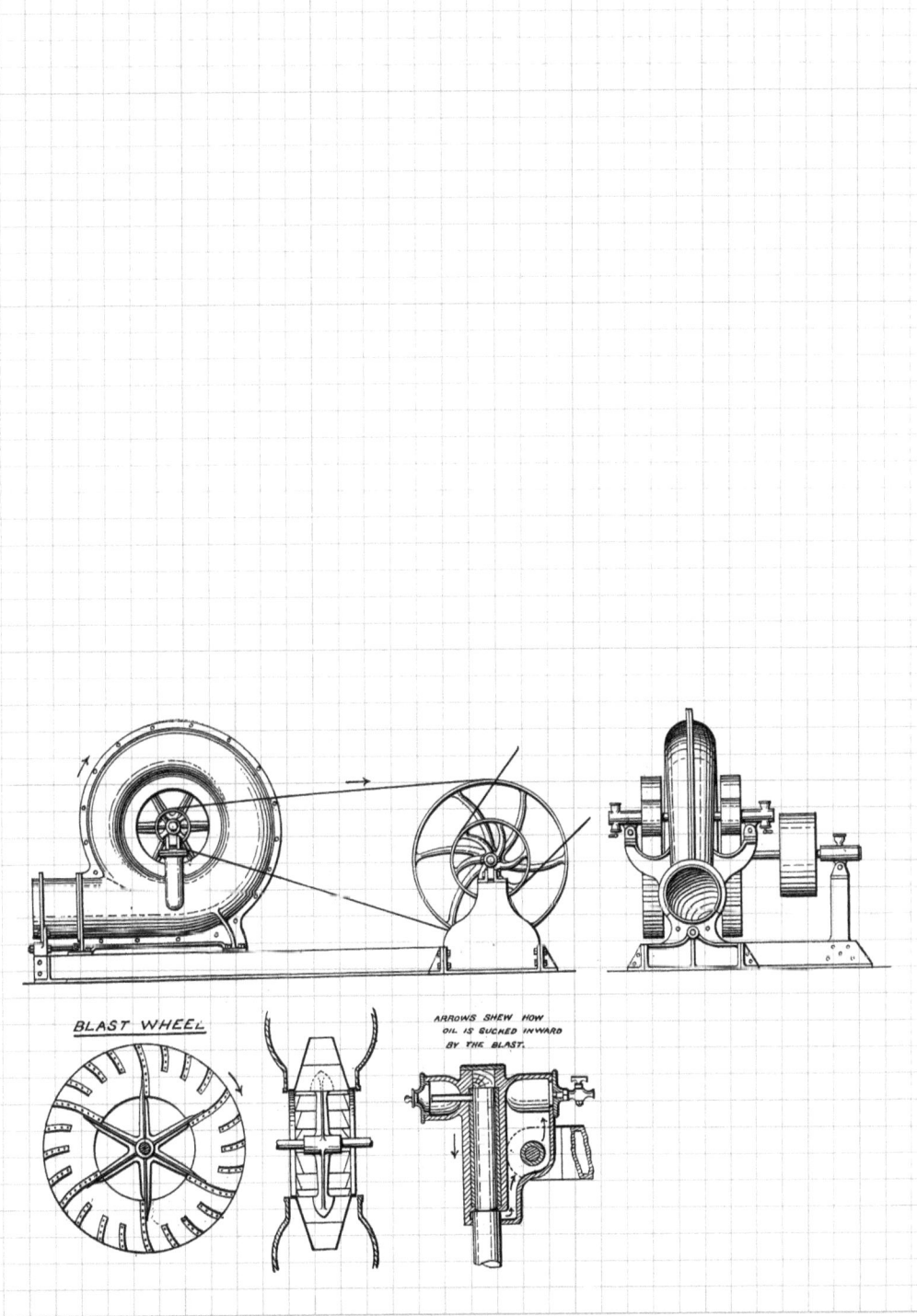

BLAST WHEEL

ARROWS SHEW HOW
OIL IS SUCKED INWARD
BY THE BLAST.

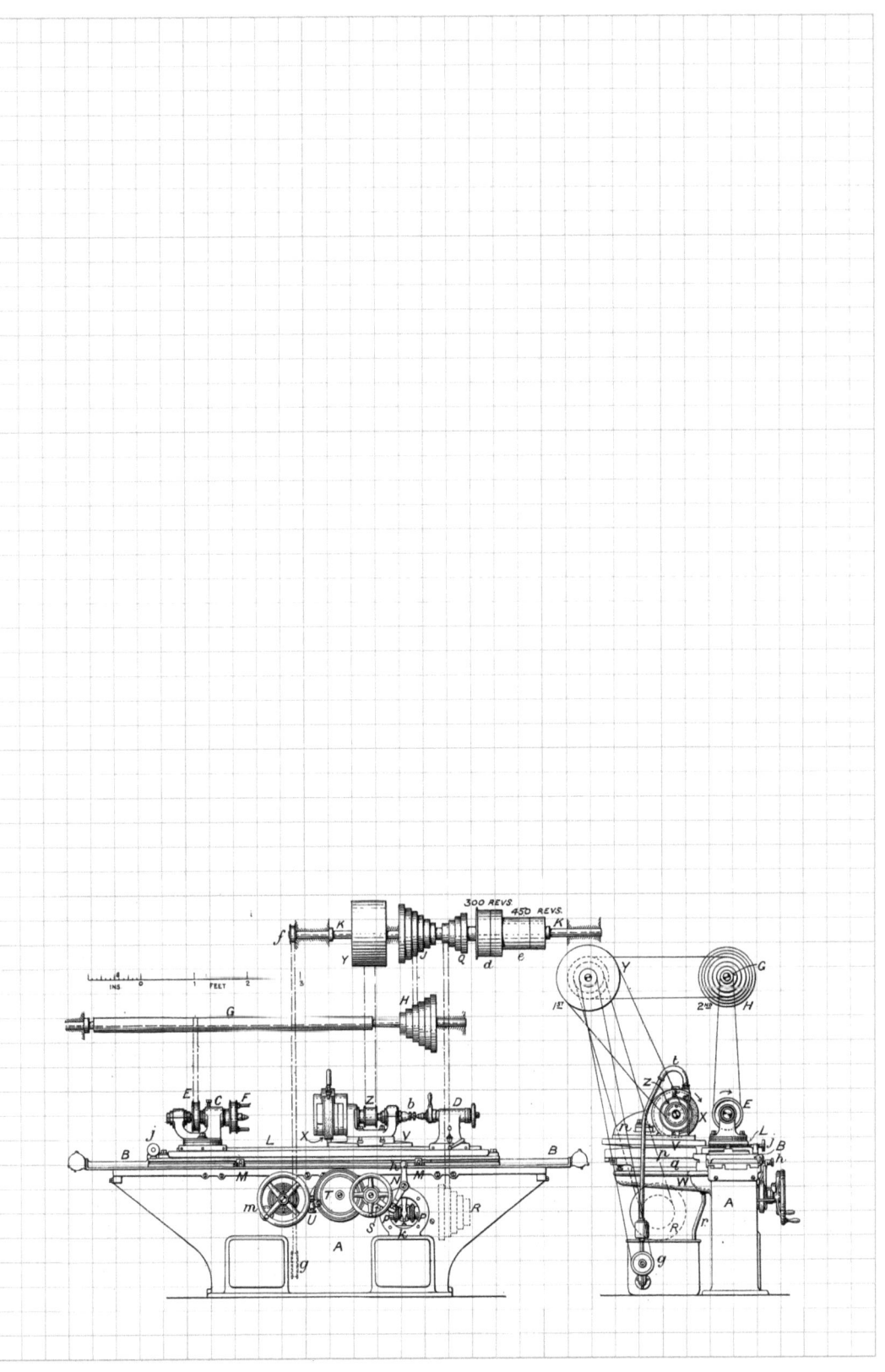

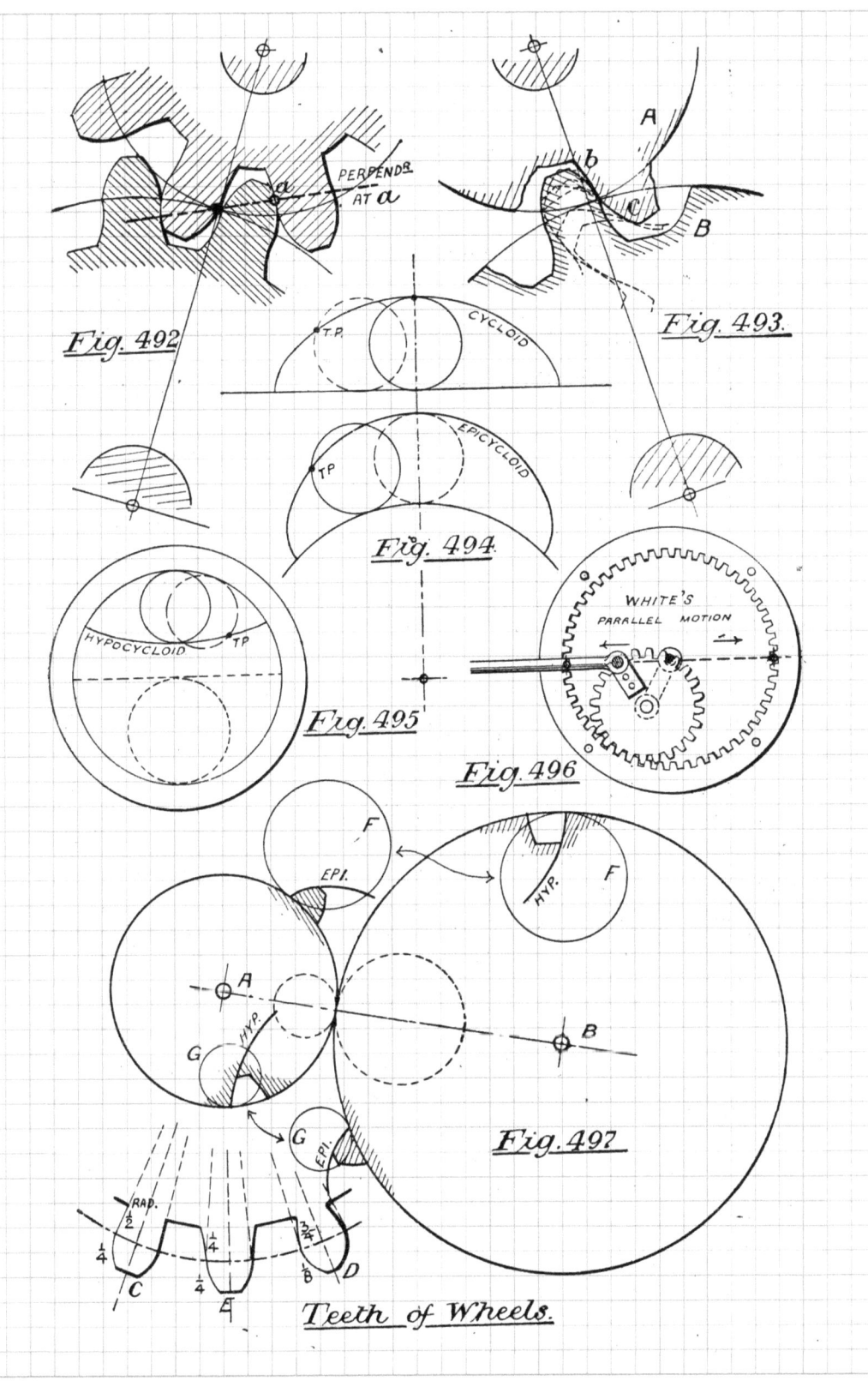

Fig. 492

Fig. 493.

PERPEND.
AT *a*

A

B

CYCLOID

T.P.

EPICYCLOID

TP

Fig. 494.

HYPOCYCLOID

TP

Fig. 495

WHITE'S PARALLEL MOTION

Fig. 496

F

EPI.

HYP.

F

A

HYP.

B

G

G

EPI.

RAD.
½

¼

¼

¼

¾
⅛

C

E

D

Fig. 497

Teeth of Wheels.

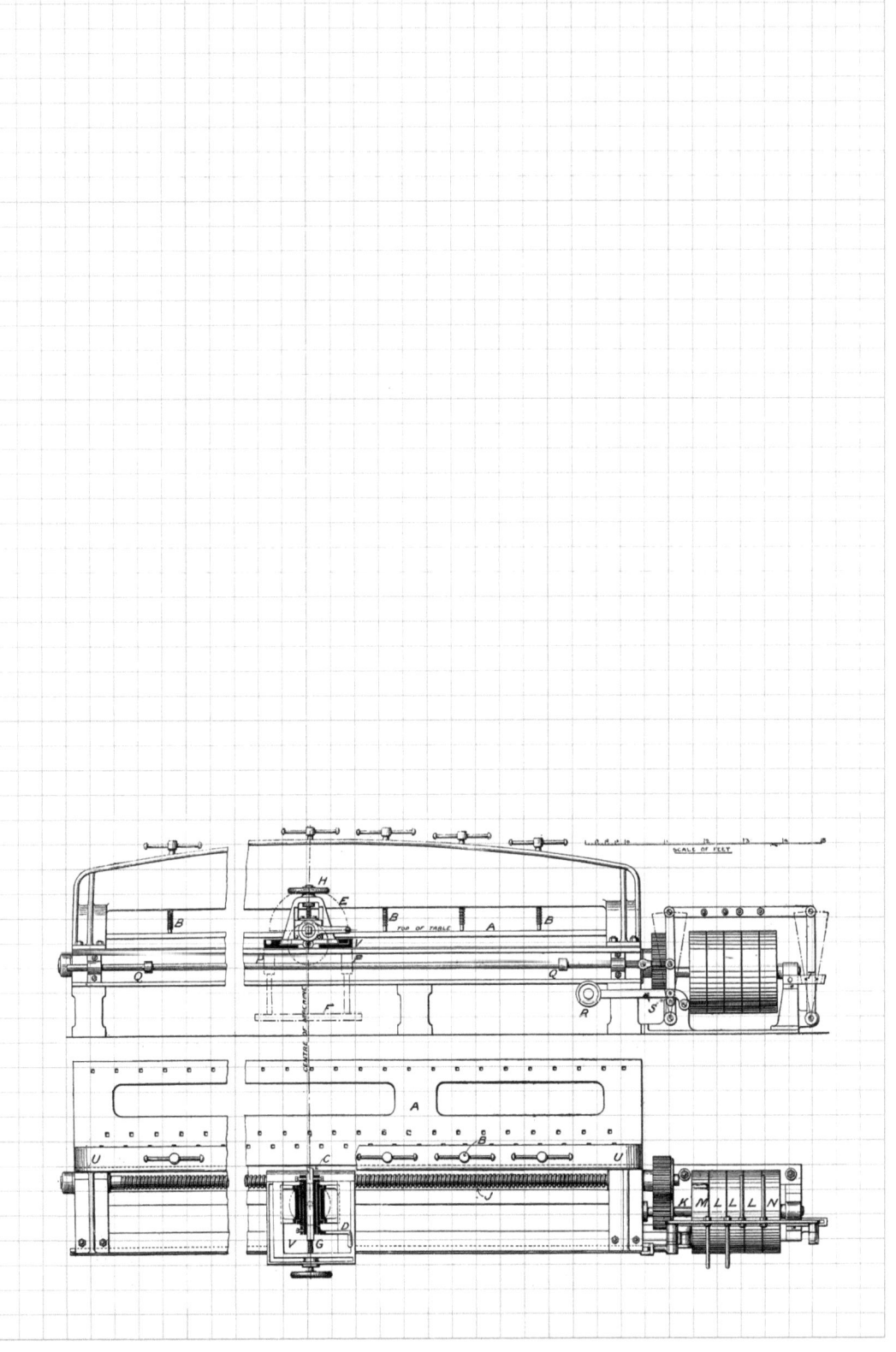

SCALE OF FEET

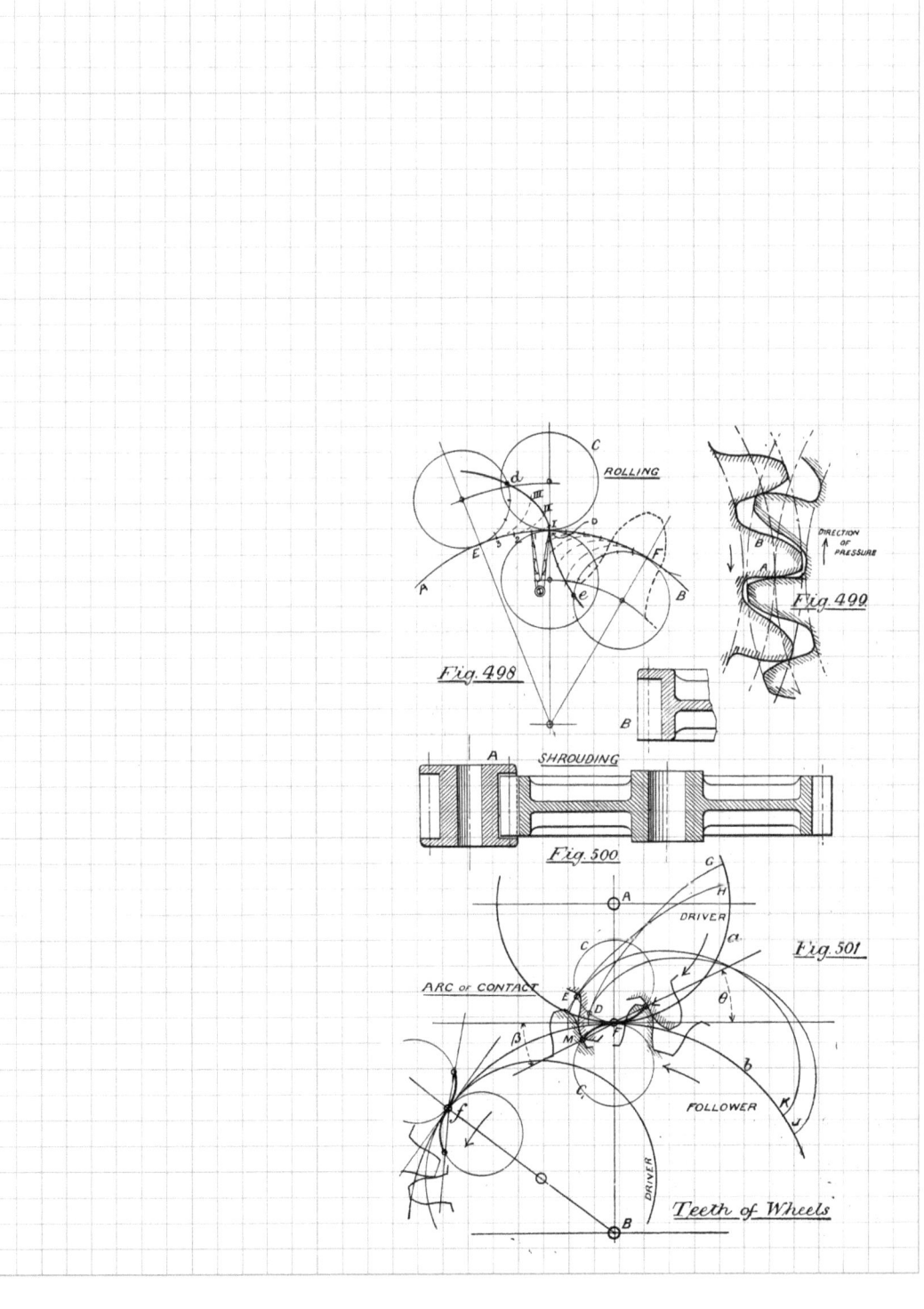

ROLLING

Fig. 498

DIRECTION OF PRESSURE

Fig. 499

SHROUDING

Fig. 500

DRIVER

ARC OF CONTACT

Fig. 501

FOLLOWER

DRIVER

Teeth of Wheels

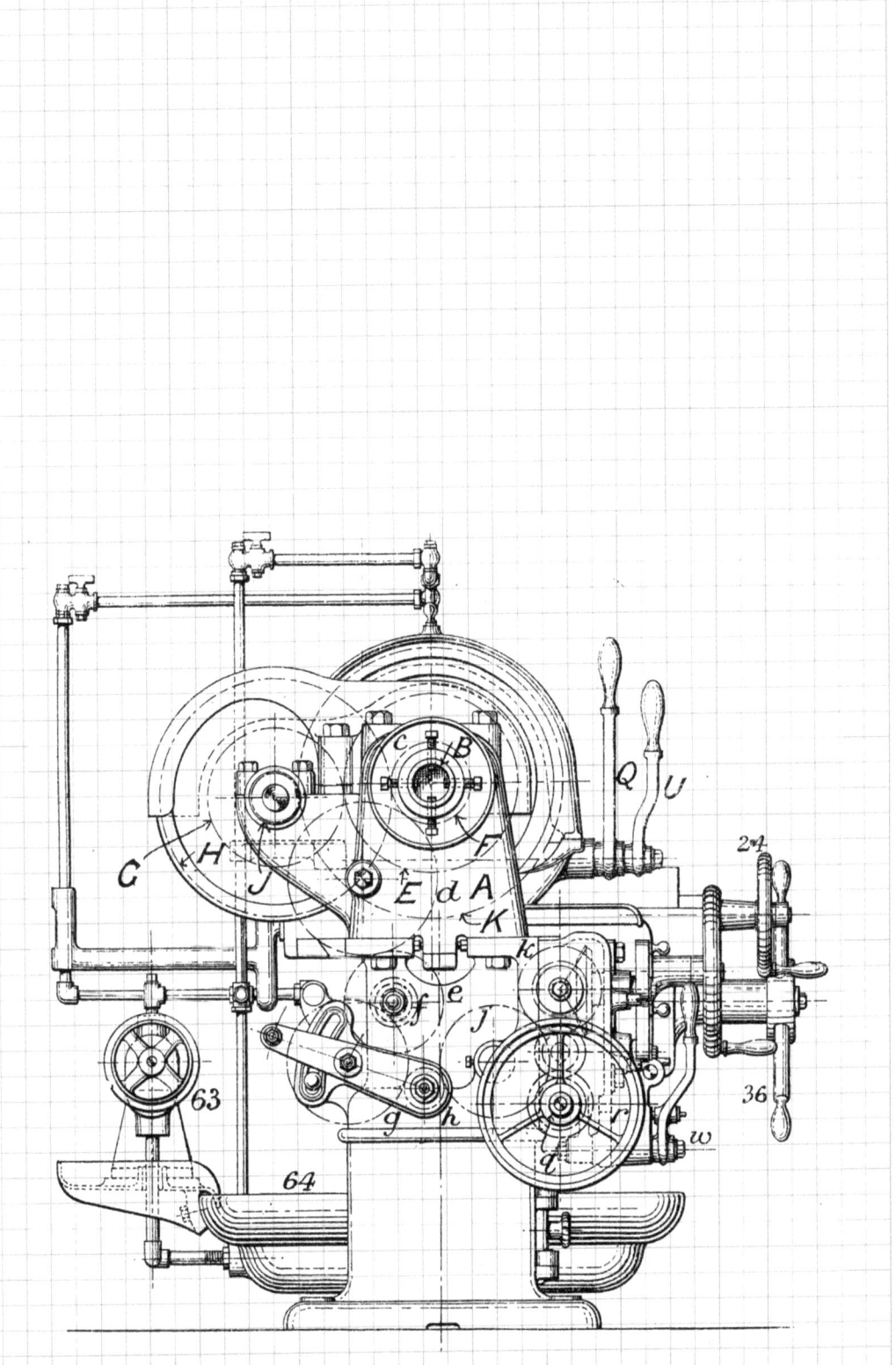

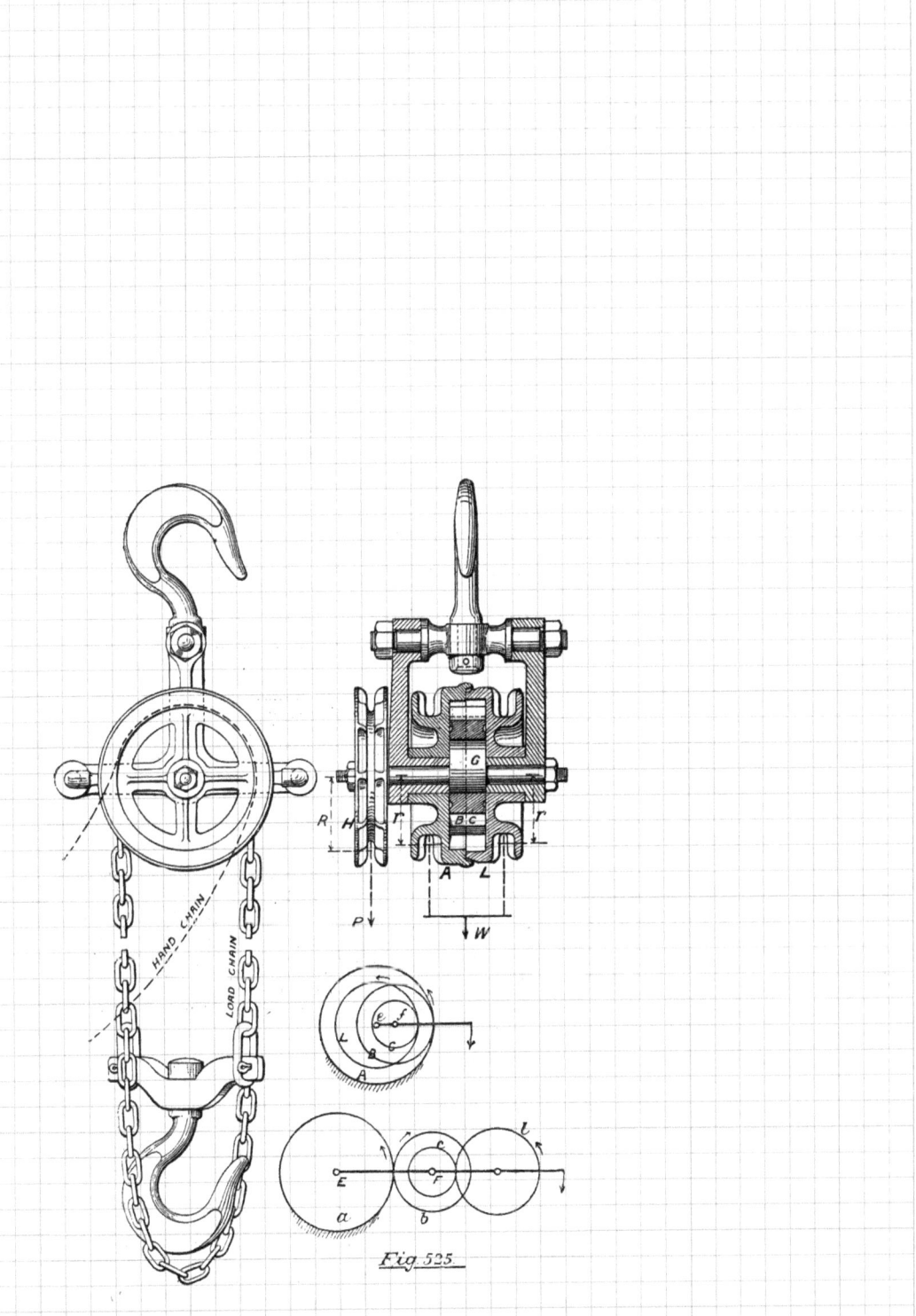

HAND CHAIN

LOAD CHAIN

Fig. 525.

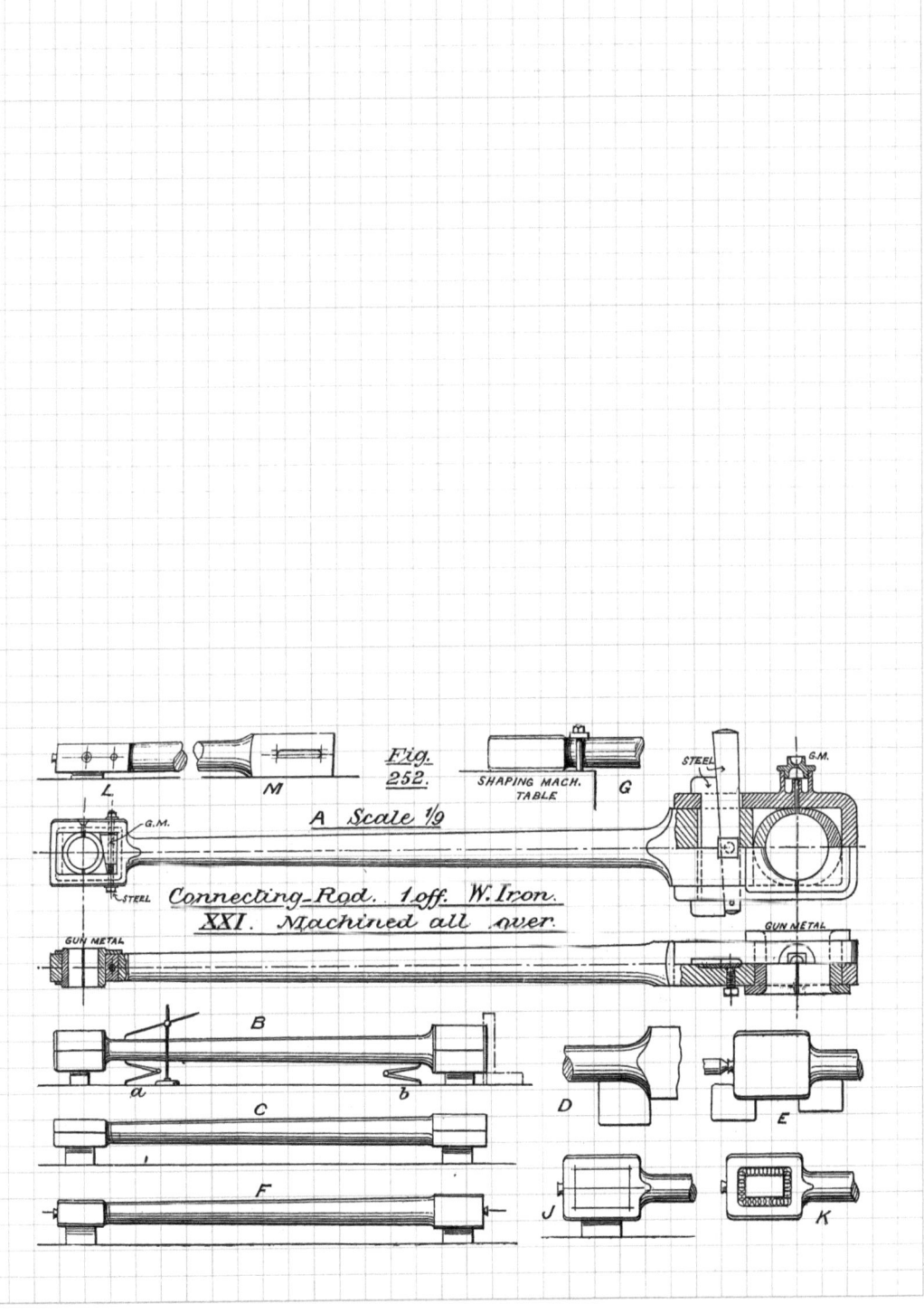

L   M   **Fig. 252.**

SHAPING MACH. TABLE   G

STEEL   G.M.

A Scale 1/9

G.M.   STEEL

Connecting-Rod. 1 off. W. Iron.
XXI. Machined all over.

GUN METAL   GUN METAL

B

a   b

C

F

D   E

J   K

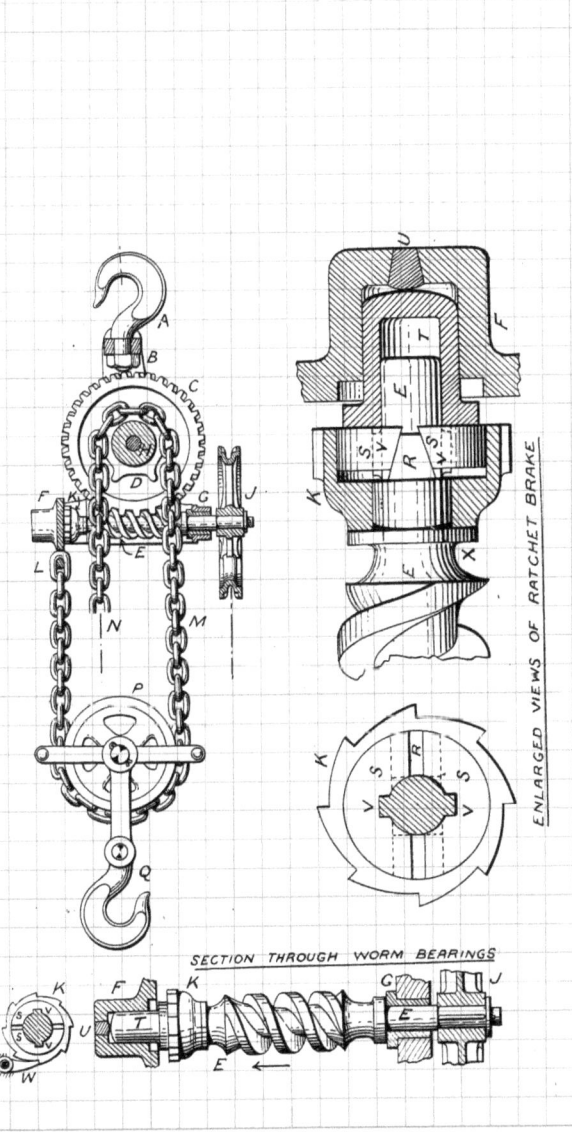

ENLARGED VIEWS OF RATCHET BRAKE

SECTION THROUGH WORM BEARINGS

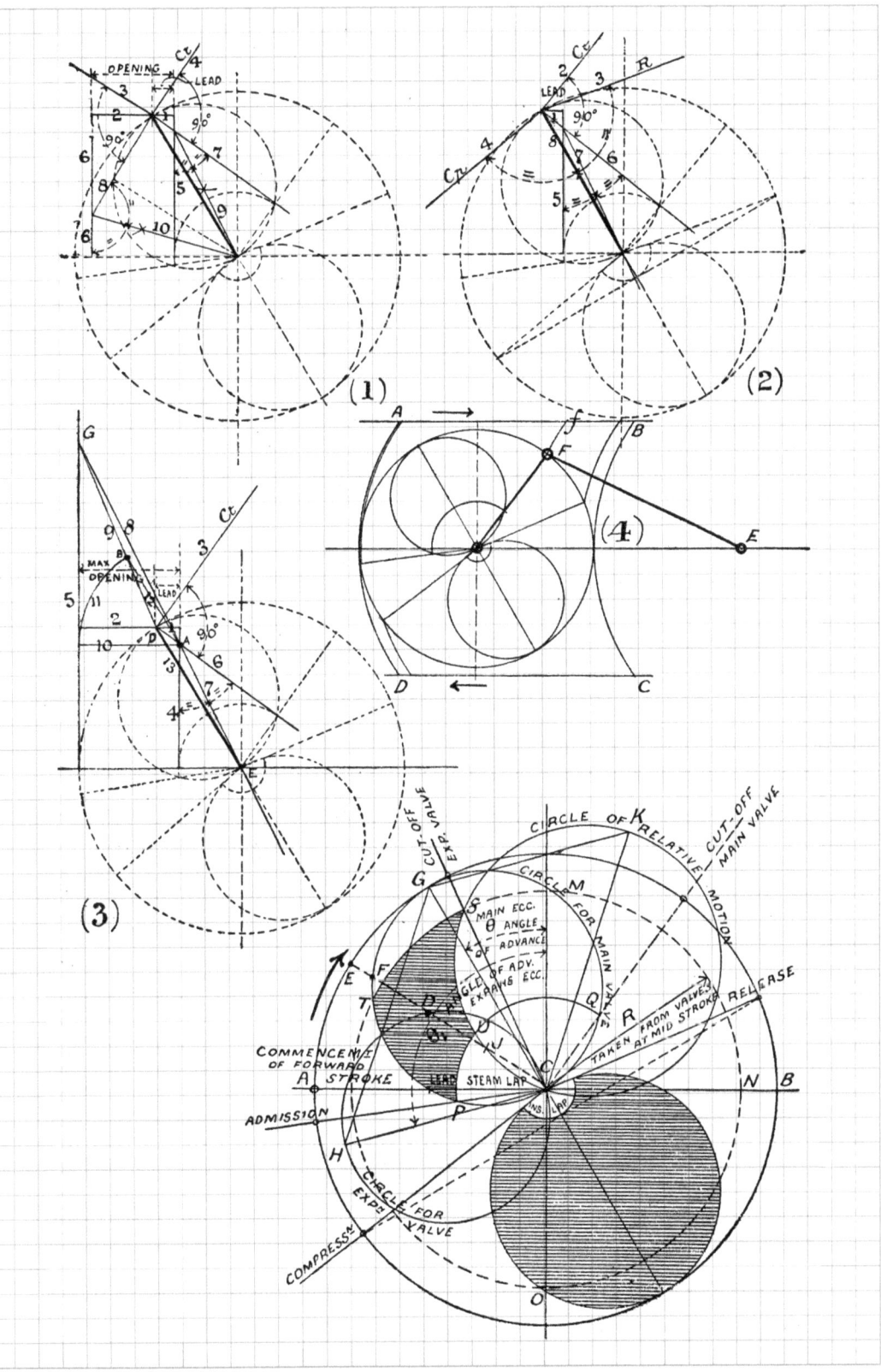

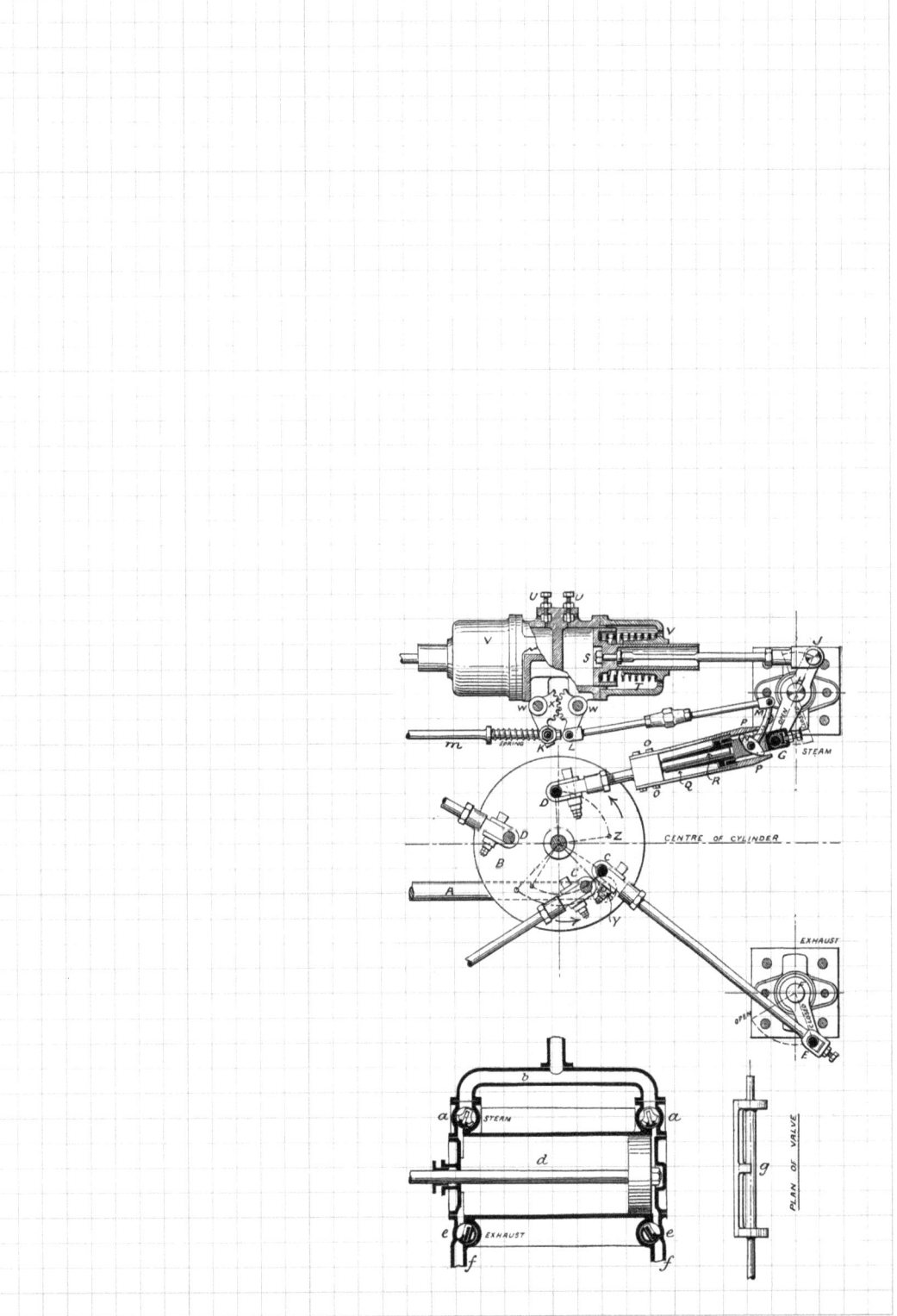

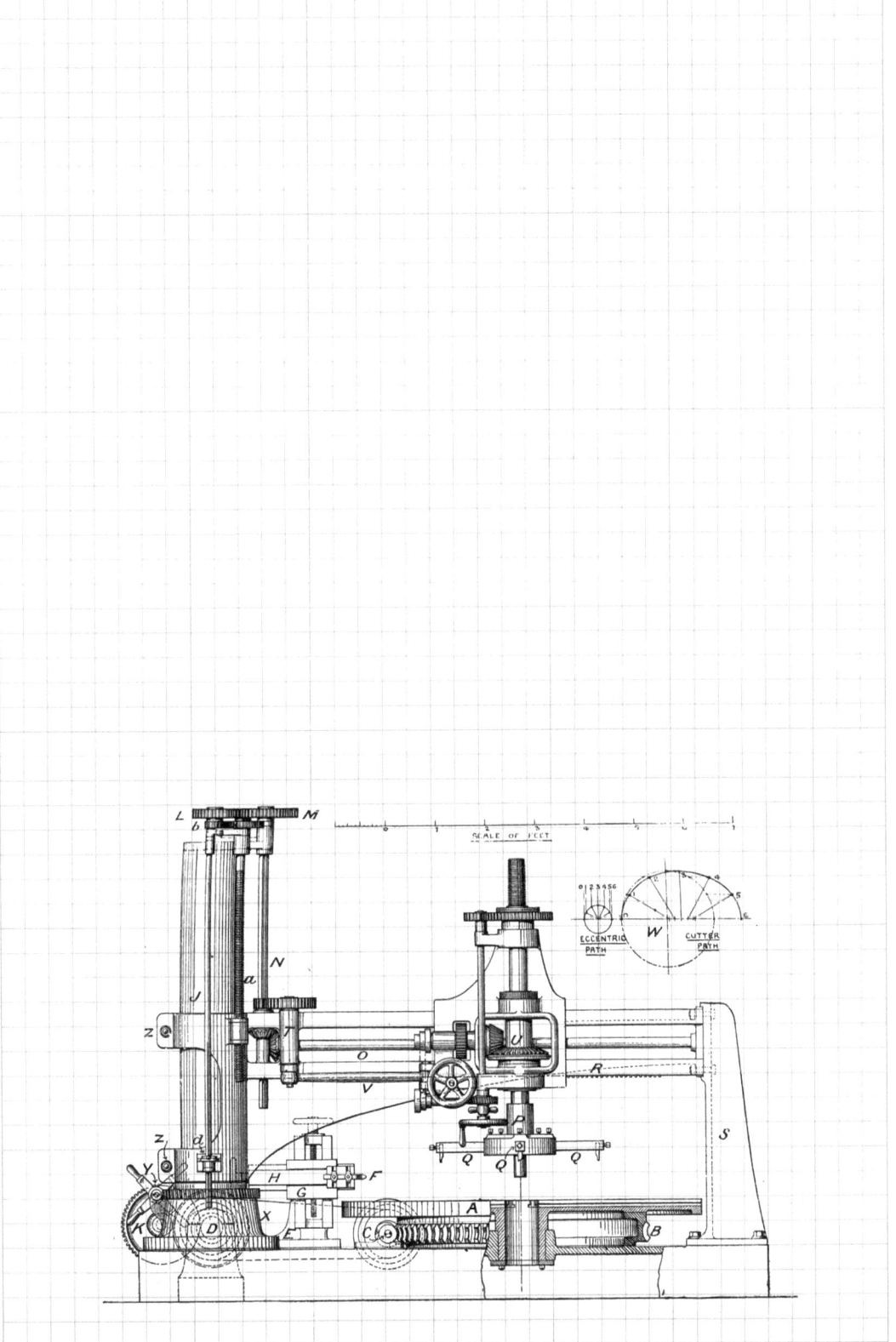

SCALE OF FEET

ECCENTRIC
PATH

CUTTER
PATH

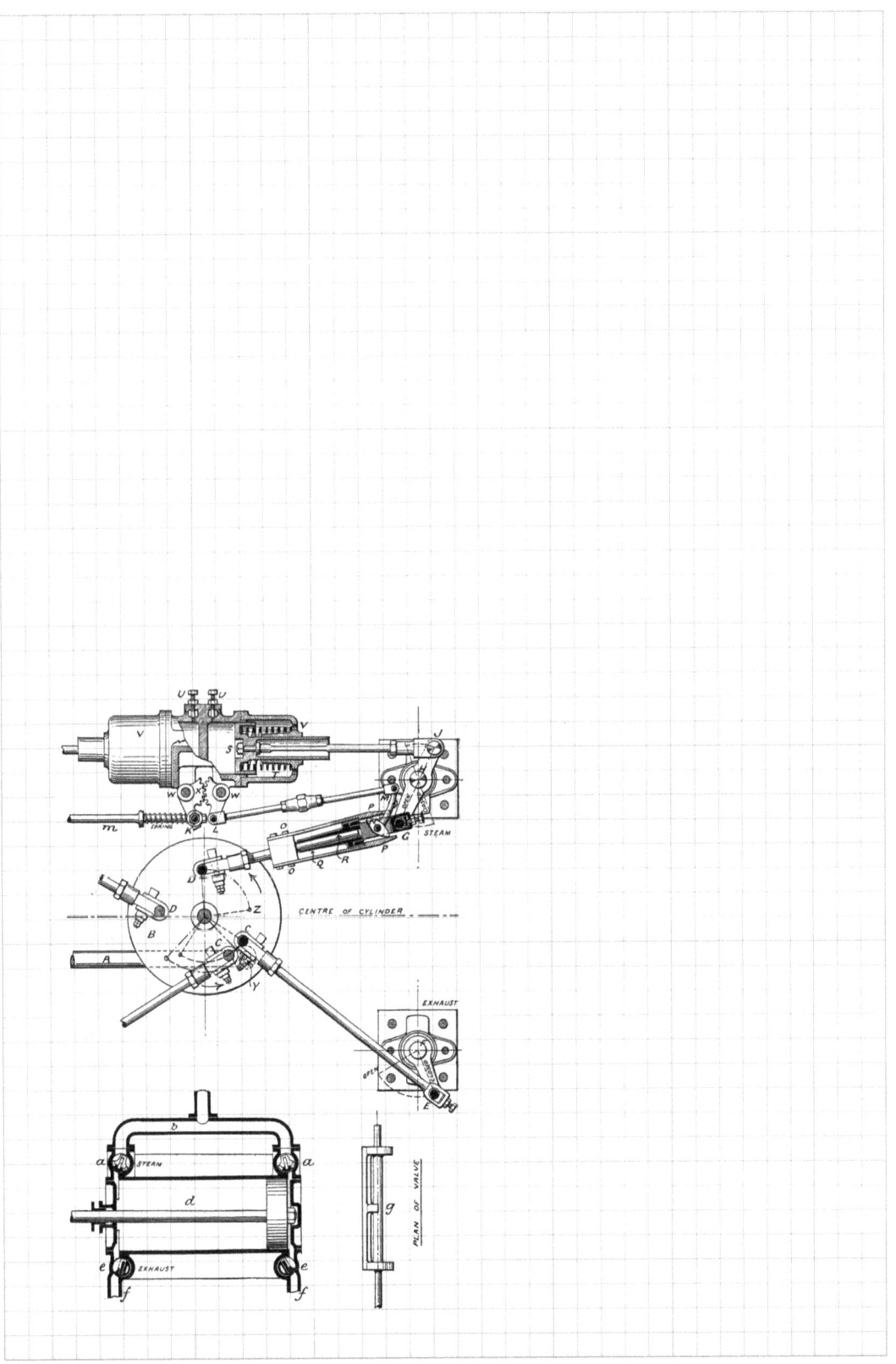

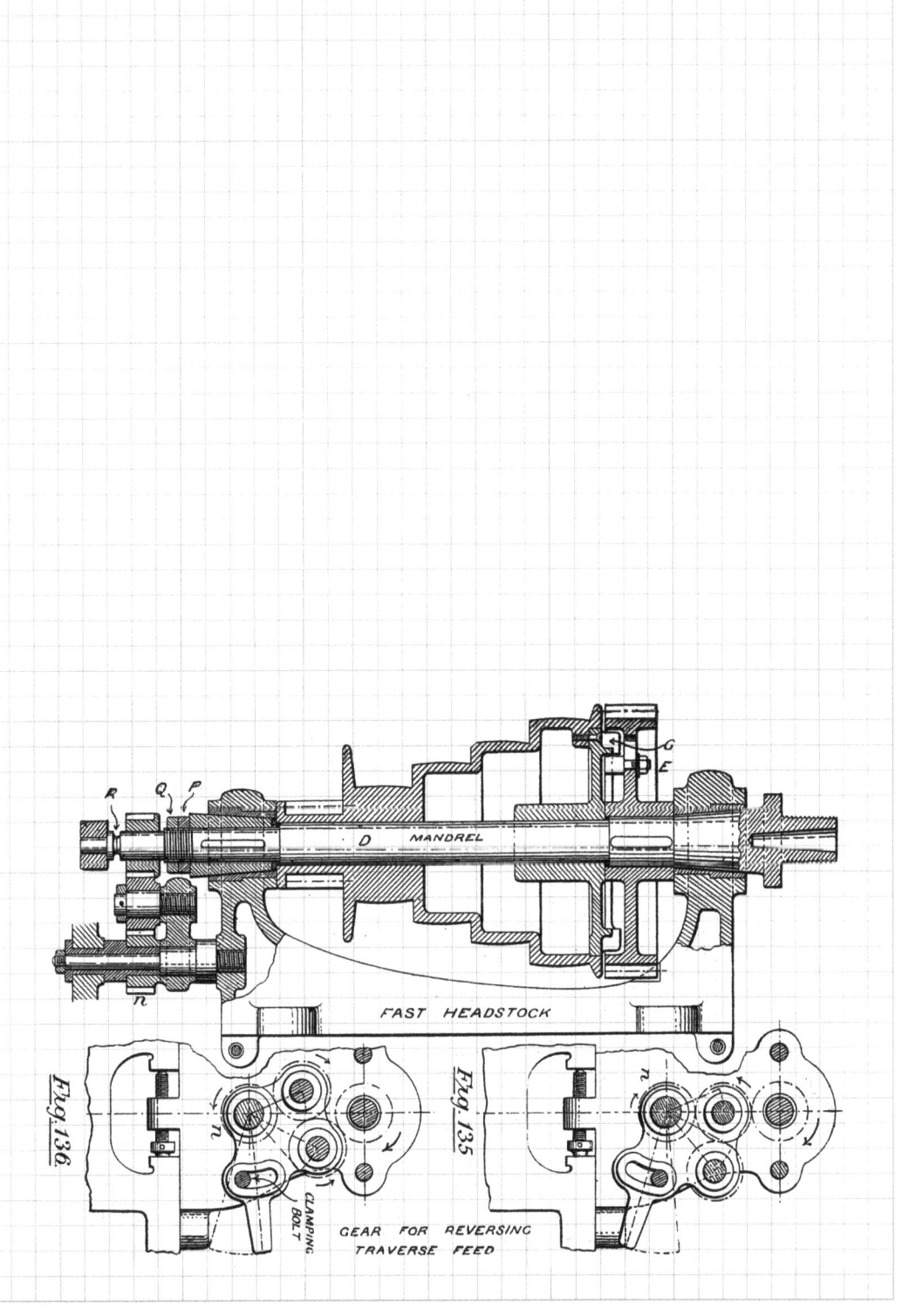

MANDREL

FAST HEADSTOCK

Fig. 136

Fig. 135

CLAMPING BOLT

GEAR FOR REVERSING
TRAVERSE FEED

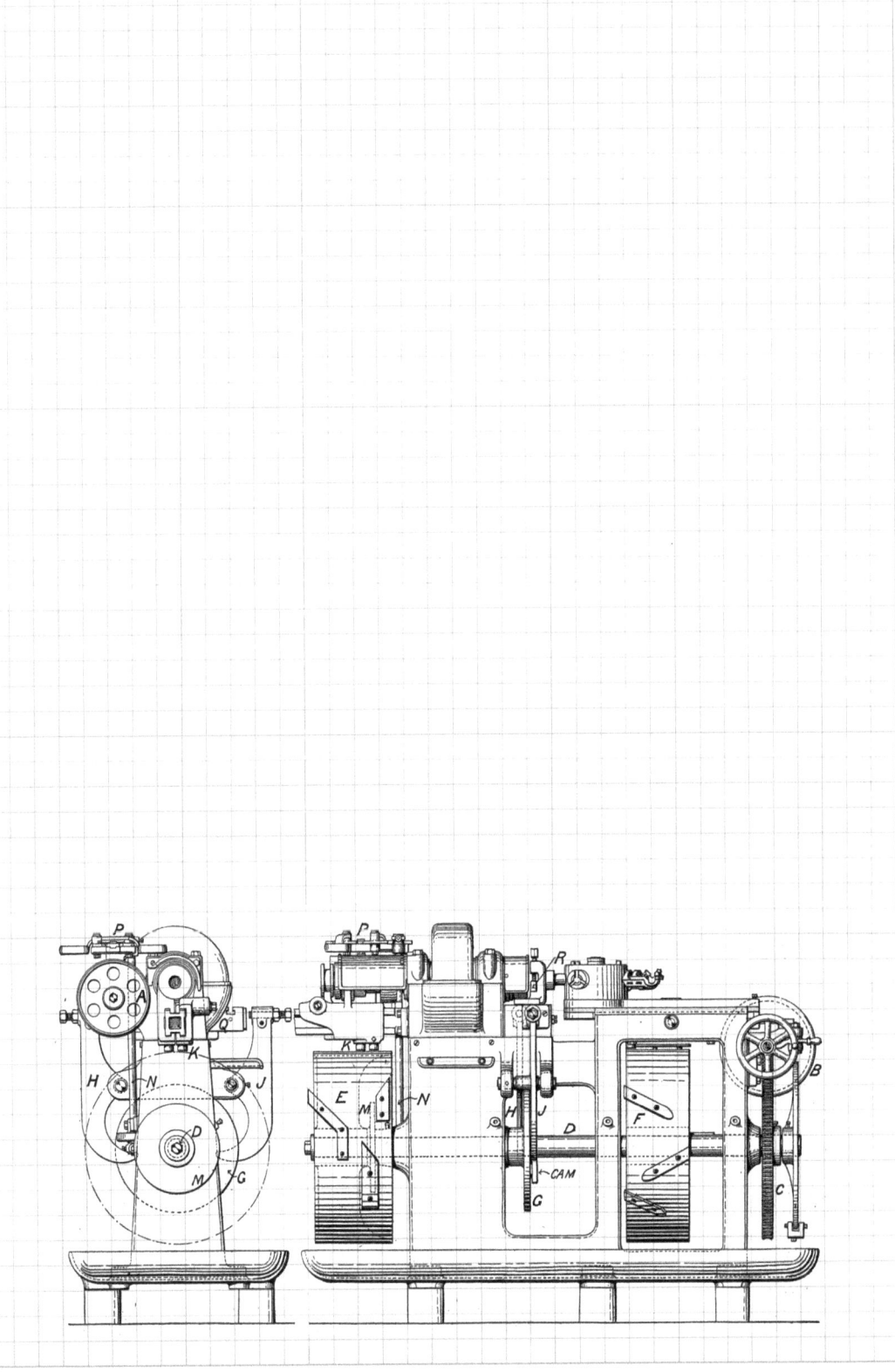

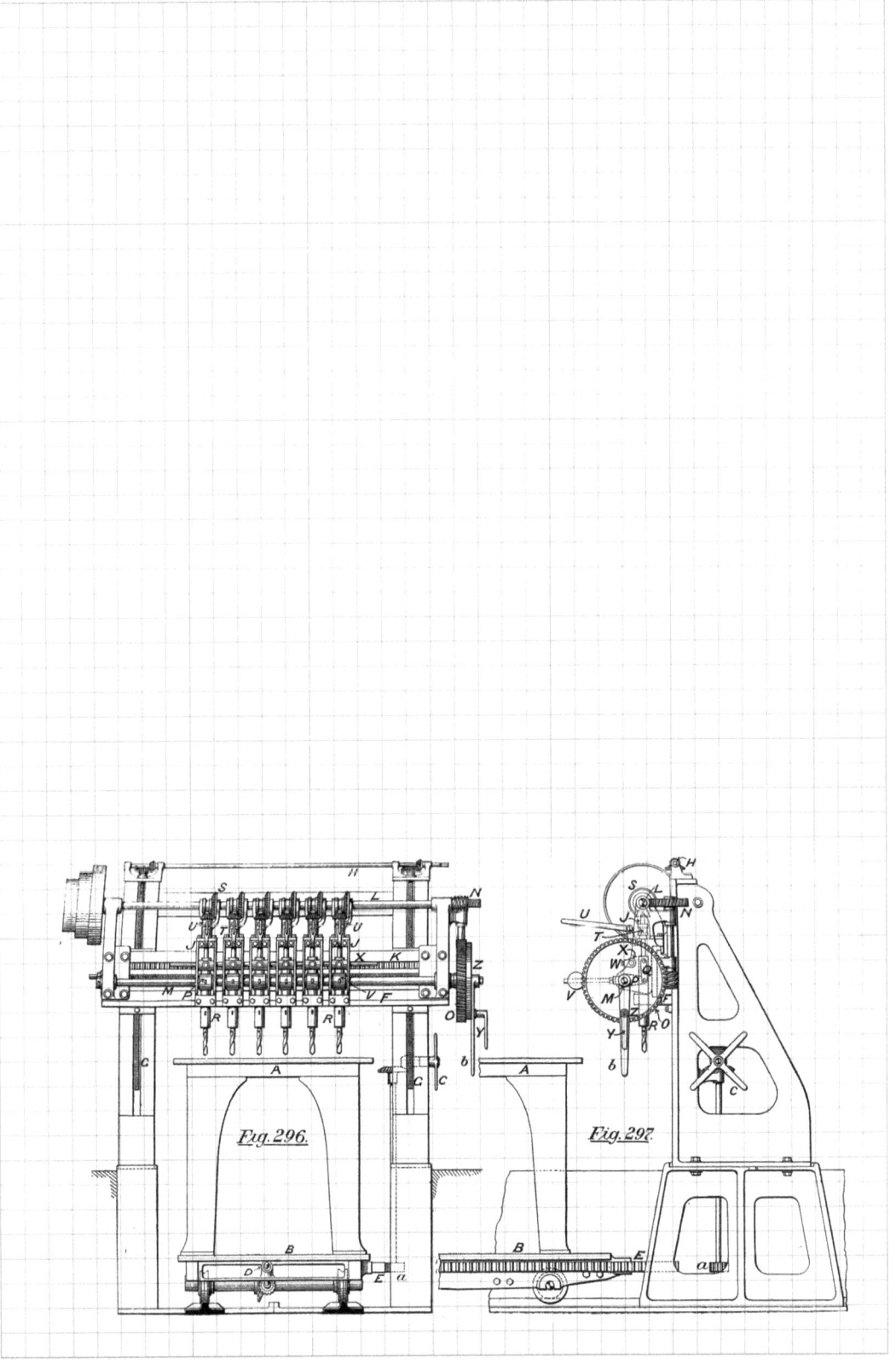

Fig. 296.

Fig. 297.

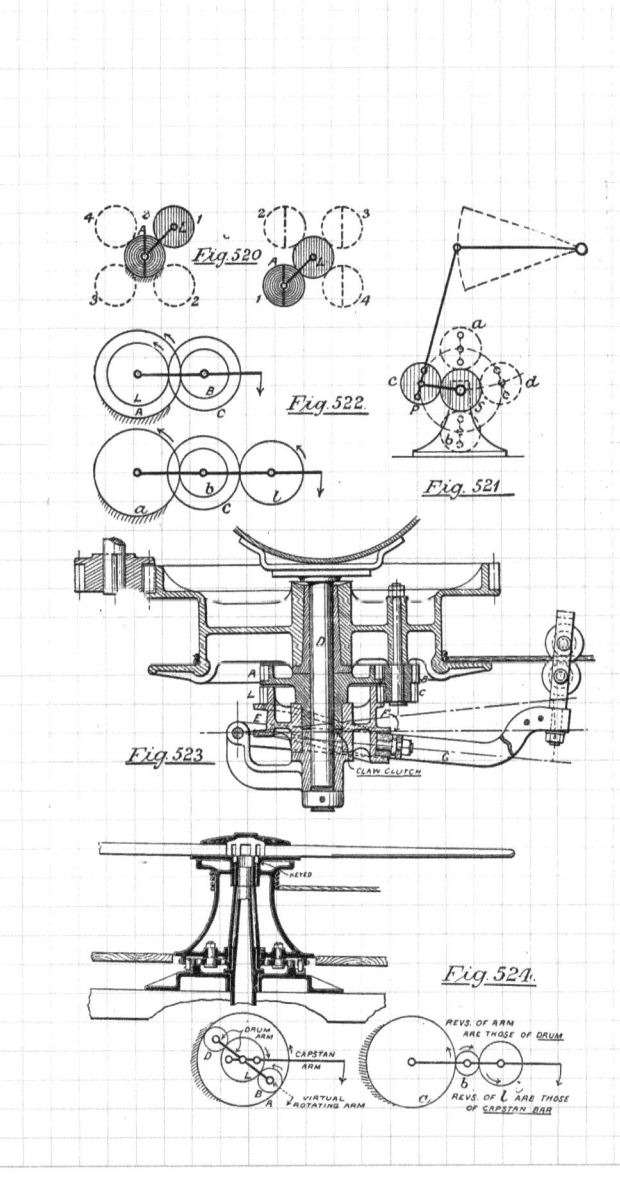

Fig.520

Fig.522

Fig. 521

Fig. 523

CLAW CLUTCH

KEYED

Fig. 524.

DRUM
ARM

CAPSTAN
ARM

VIRTUAL
ROTATING ARM

REVS. OF ARM
ARE THOSE OF DRUM

REVS. OF *b* ARE THOSE
OF CAPSTAN BAR

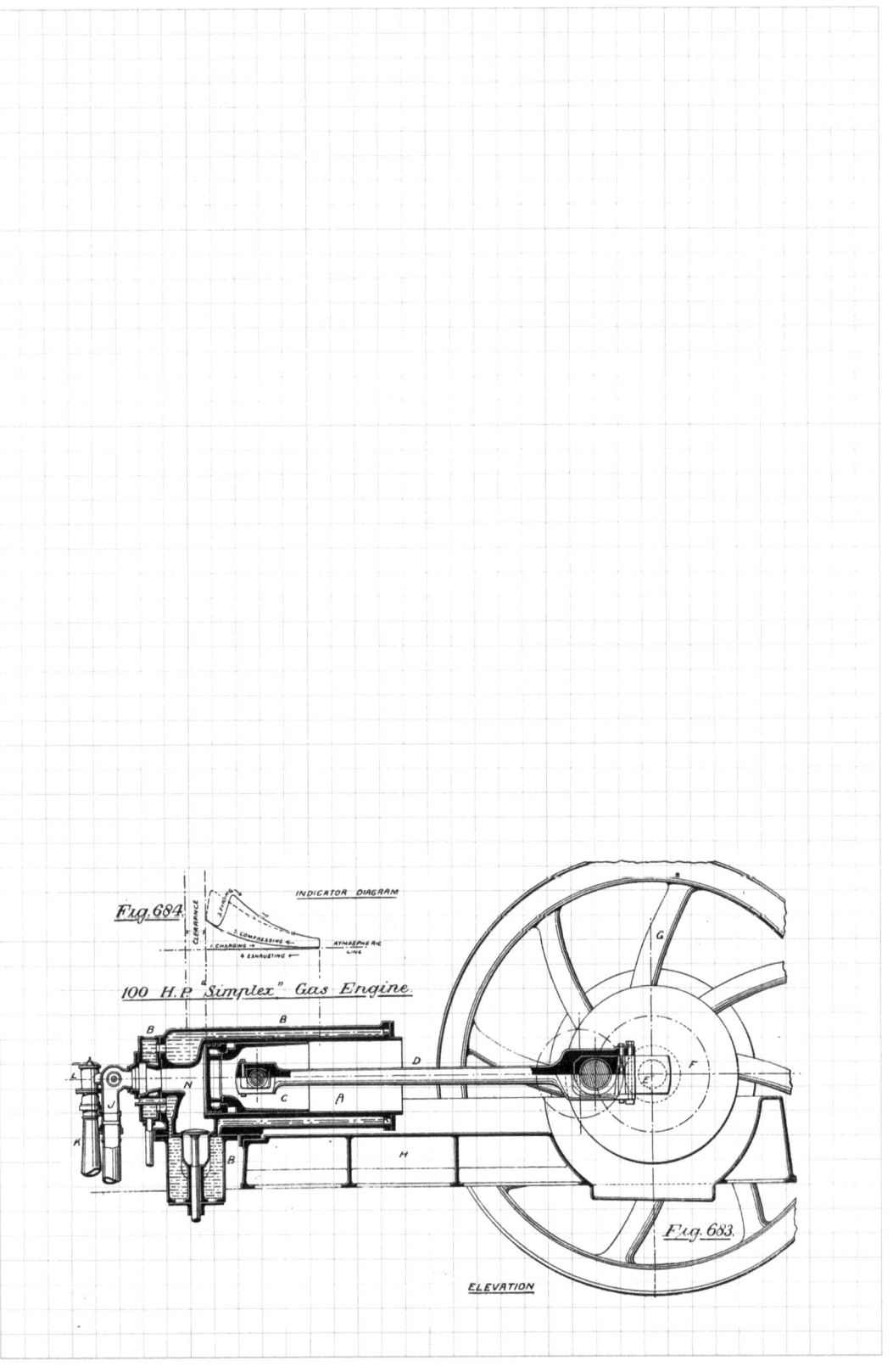

Fig. 684.

INDICATOR DIAGRAM

CLEARANCE

1 FIRING
2 COMPRESSING
3 CHARGING
4 EXHAUSTING

ATMOSPHERIC
LINE

100 H.P. "Simplex" Gas Engine

Fig. 683.

ELEVATION

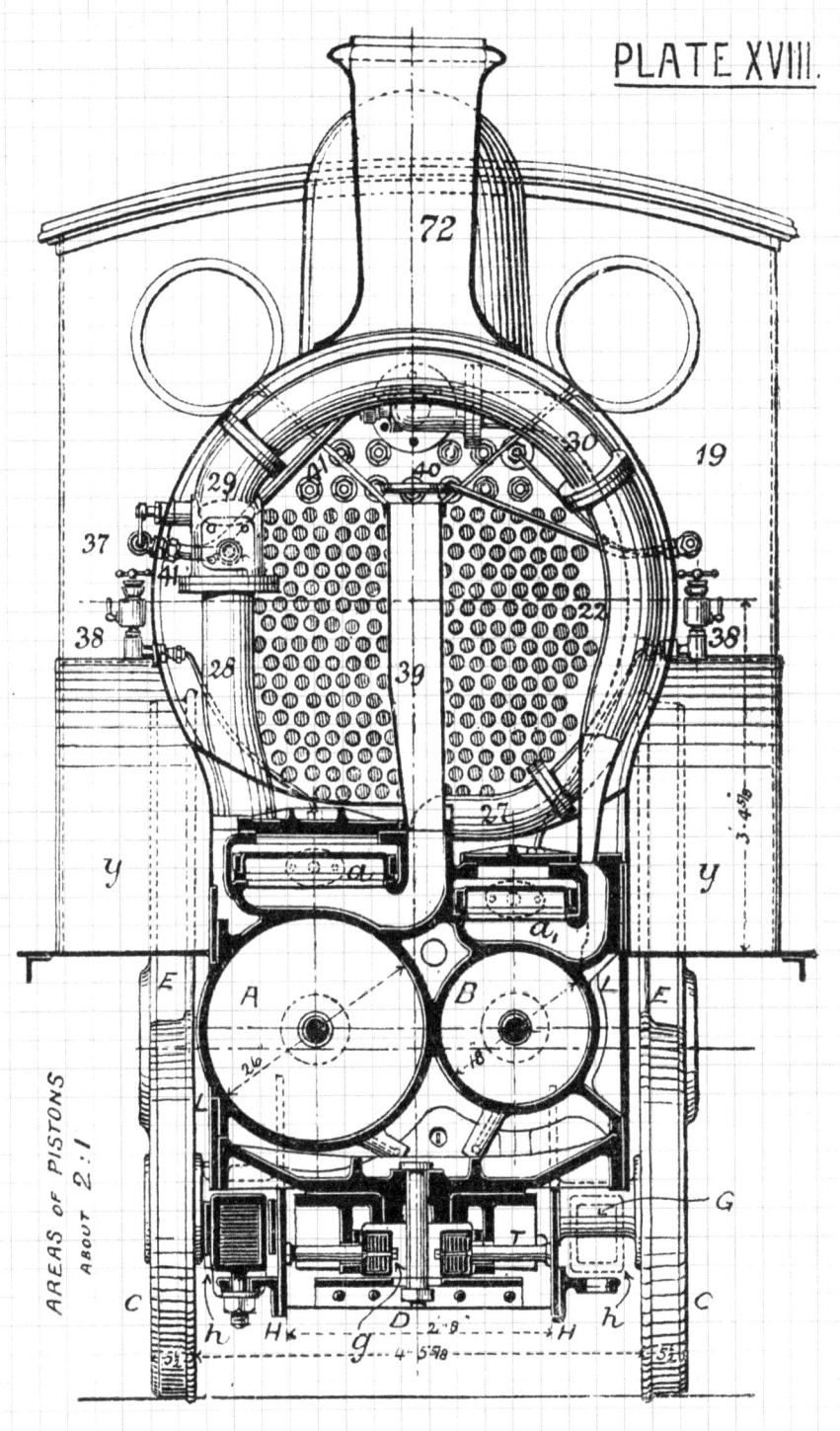

PLATE XVIII.

Fig. 677.

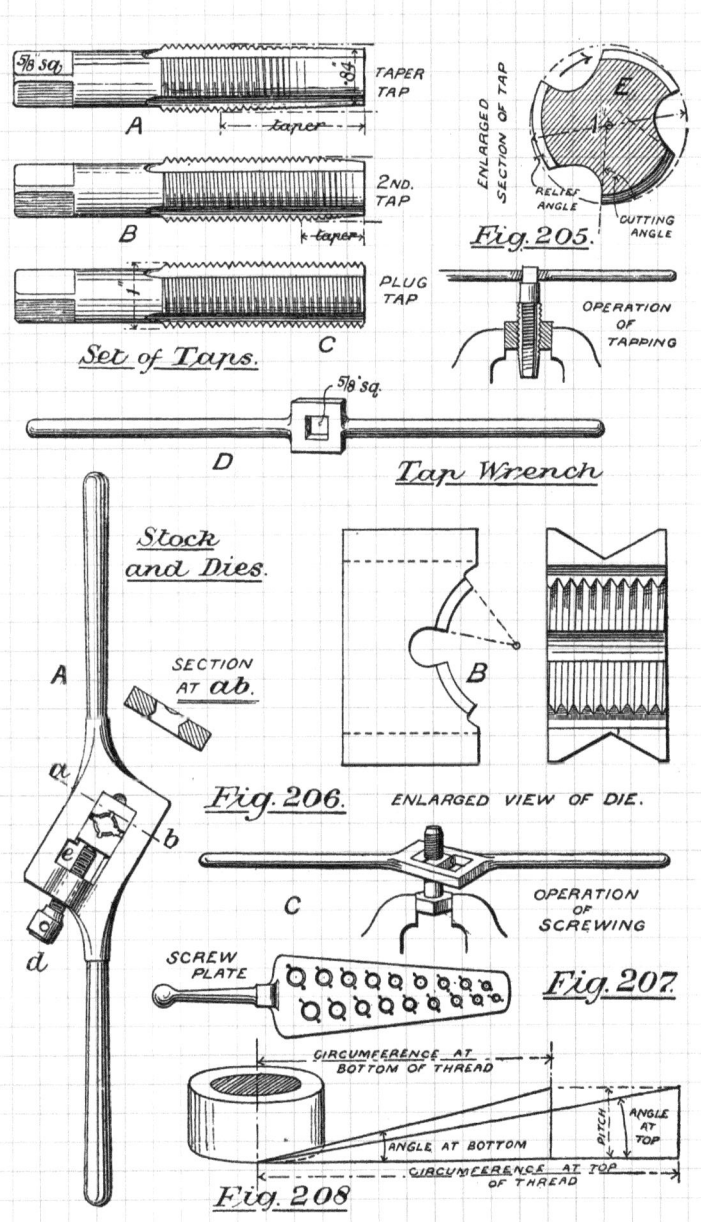

⅝ sq.

TAPER
TAP

A taper

2ND.
TAP

B taper

PLUG
TAP

C

Set of Taps.

ENLARGED SECTION OF TAP

E

RELIEF ANGLE

CUTTING ANGLE

Fig. 205.

OPERATION OF TAPPING

⅝ sq.

D Tap Wrench

Stock and Dies.

A

SECTION AT ab.

a

e

b

d

B

Fig. 206. ENLARGED VIEW OF DIE.

C OPERATION OF SCREWING

Fig. 207.

SCREW PLATE

CIRCUMFERENCE AT BOTTOM OF THREAD

ANGLE AT TOP

PITCH

ANGLE AT BOTTOM

CIRCUMFERENCE AT TOP OF THREAD

Fig. 208

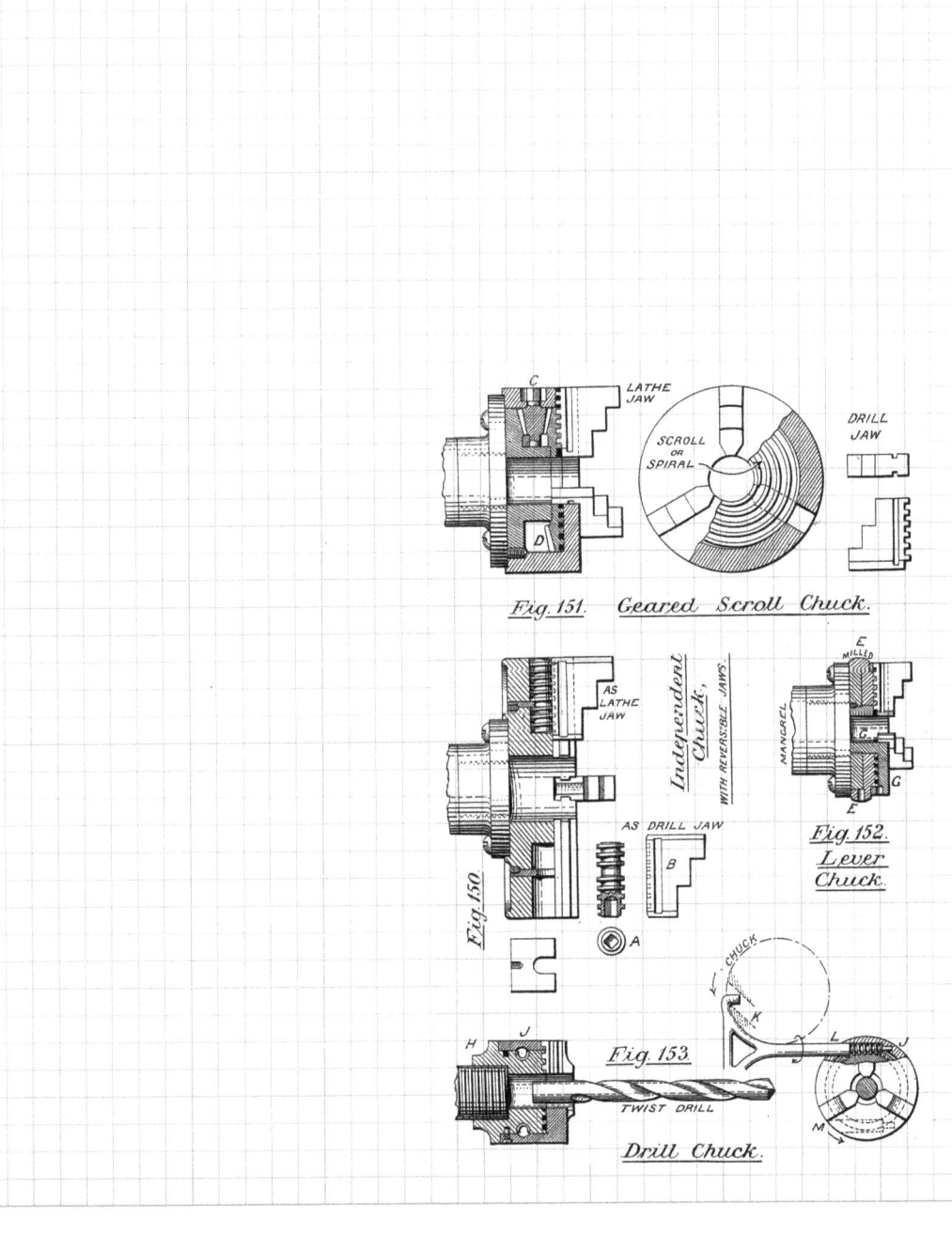

LATHE JAW

C

SCROLL OR SPIRAL

DRILL JAW

D

Fig. 151. Geared Scroll Chuck.

Independent Chuck, WITH REVERSABLE JAWS.

AS LATHE JAW

AS DRILL JAW

B

A

Fig. 150

E MILLED

MANDREL

E

G

Fig. 152. Lever Chuck.

CHUCK

K

L

J

H J

Fig. 153.

TWIST DRILL

M

Drill Chuck.

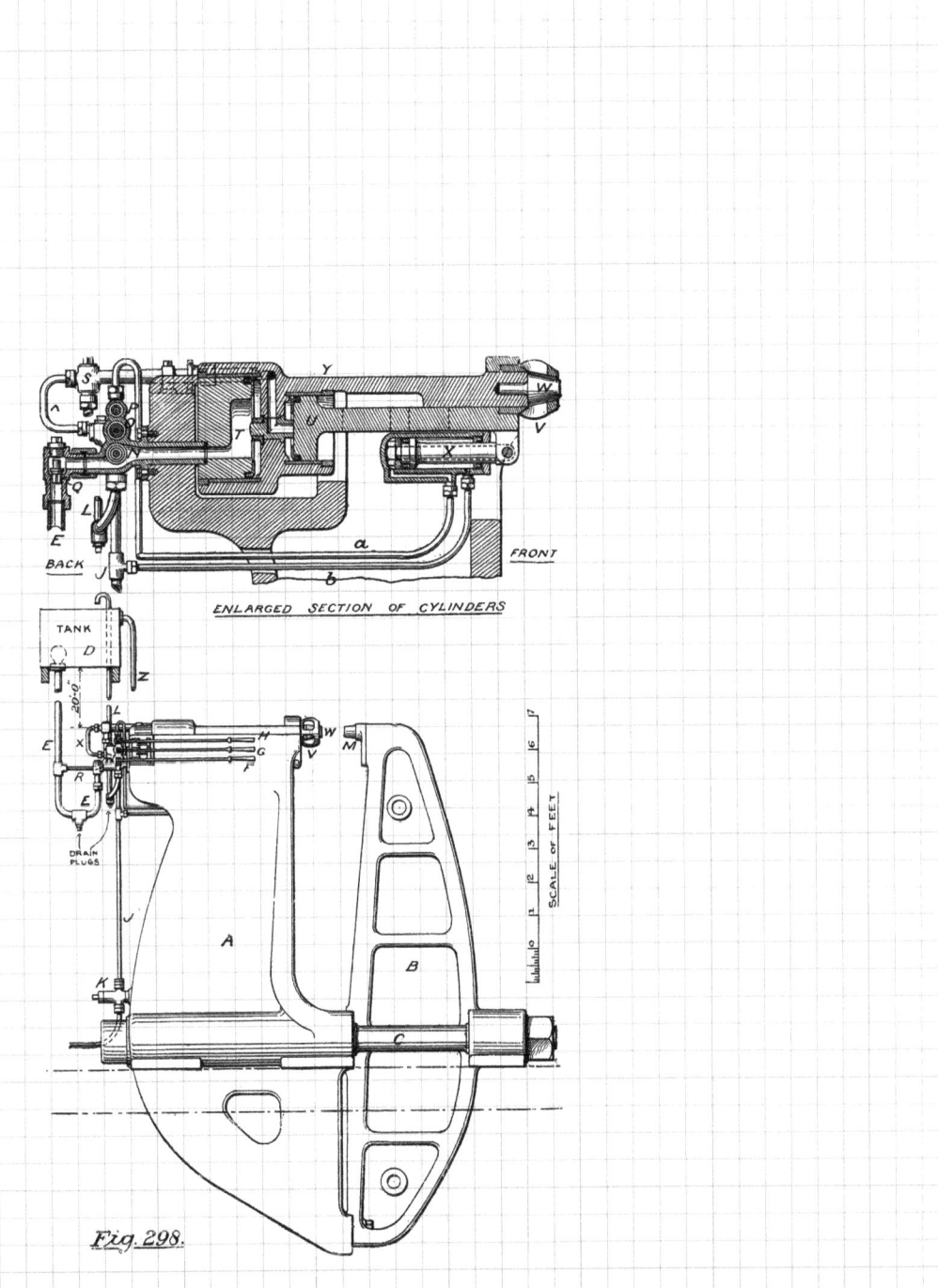

ENLARGED SECTION OF CYLINDERS

SCALE OF FEET

Fig. 298.

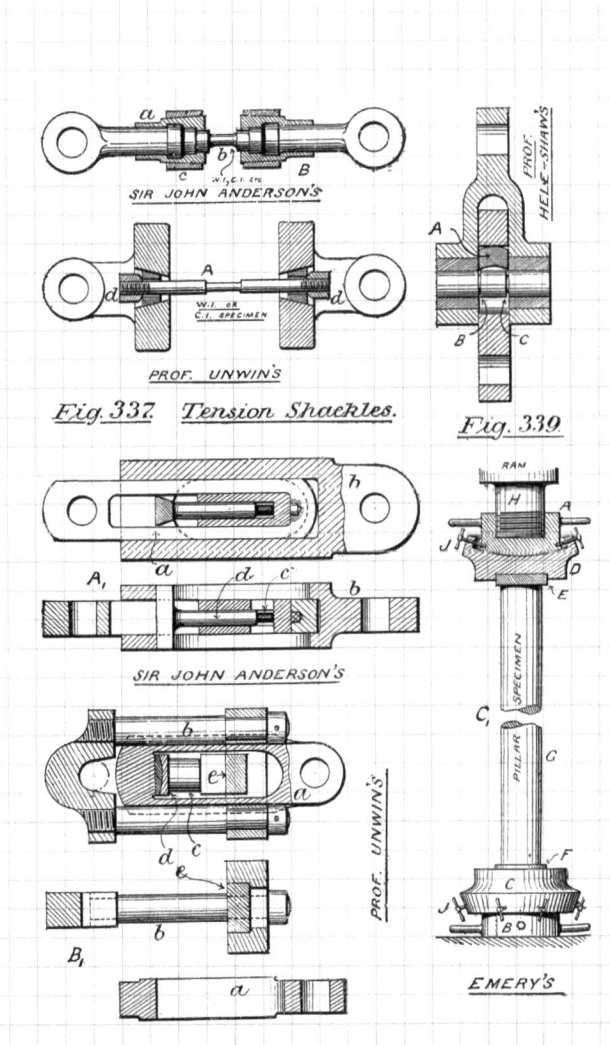

SIR JOHN ANDERSON'S

W.I. OR C.I. SPECIMEN

PROF. UNWIN'S

Fig. 337. *Tension Shackles.*

Fig. 339.

PROF. HELE-SHAW'S

SIR JOHN ANDERSON'S

PROF. UNWIN'S

EMERY'S

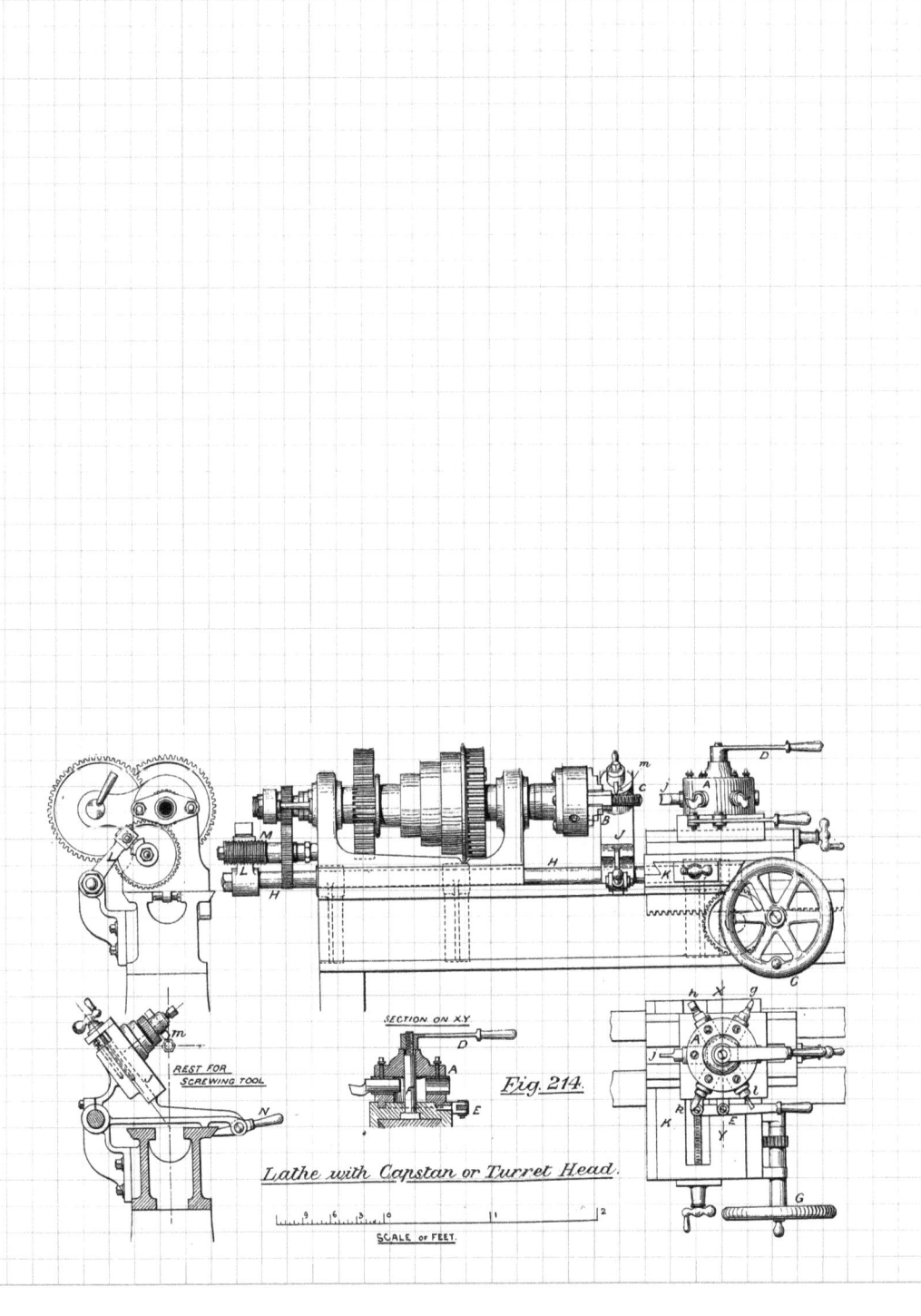

REST FOR
SCREWING TOOL

SECTION ON X.Y

Fig. 214.

Lathe with Capstan or Turret Head.

SCALE of FEET.

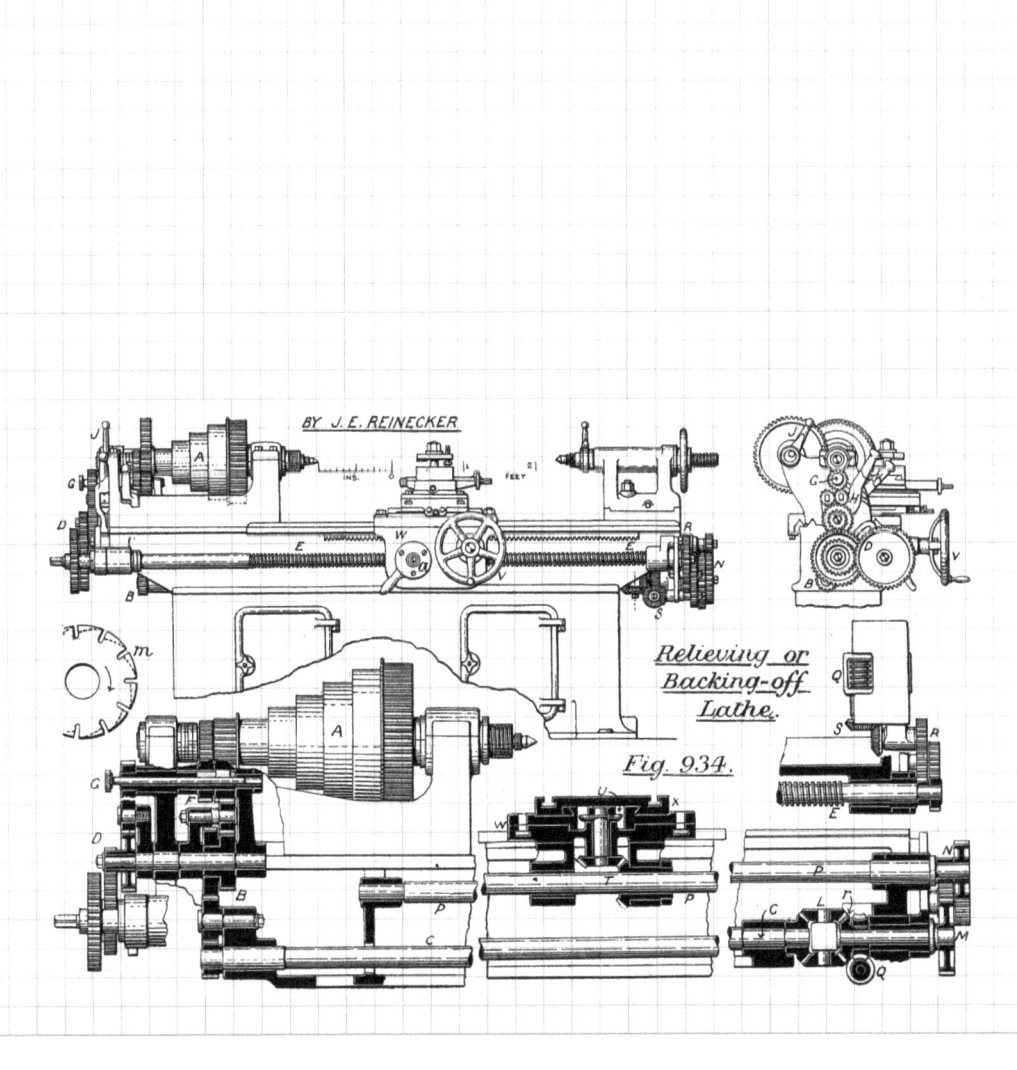

BY J.E. REINECKER

Relieving or
Backing-off
Lathe.

Fig. 934.

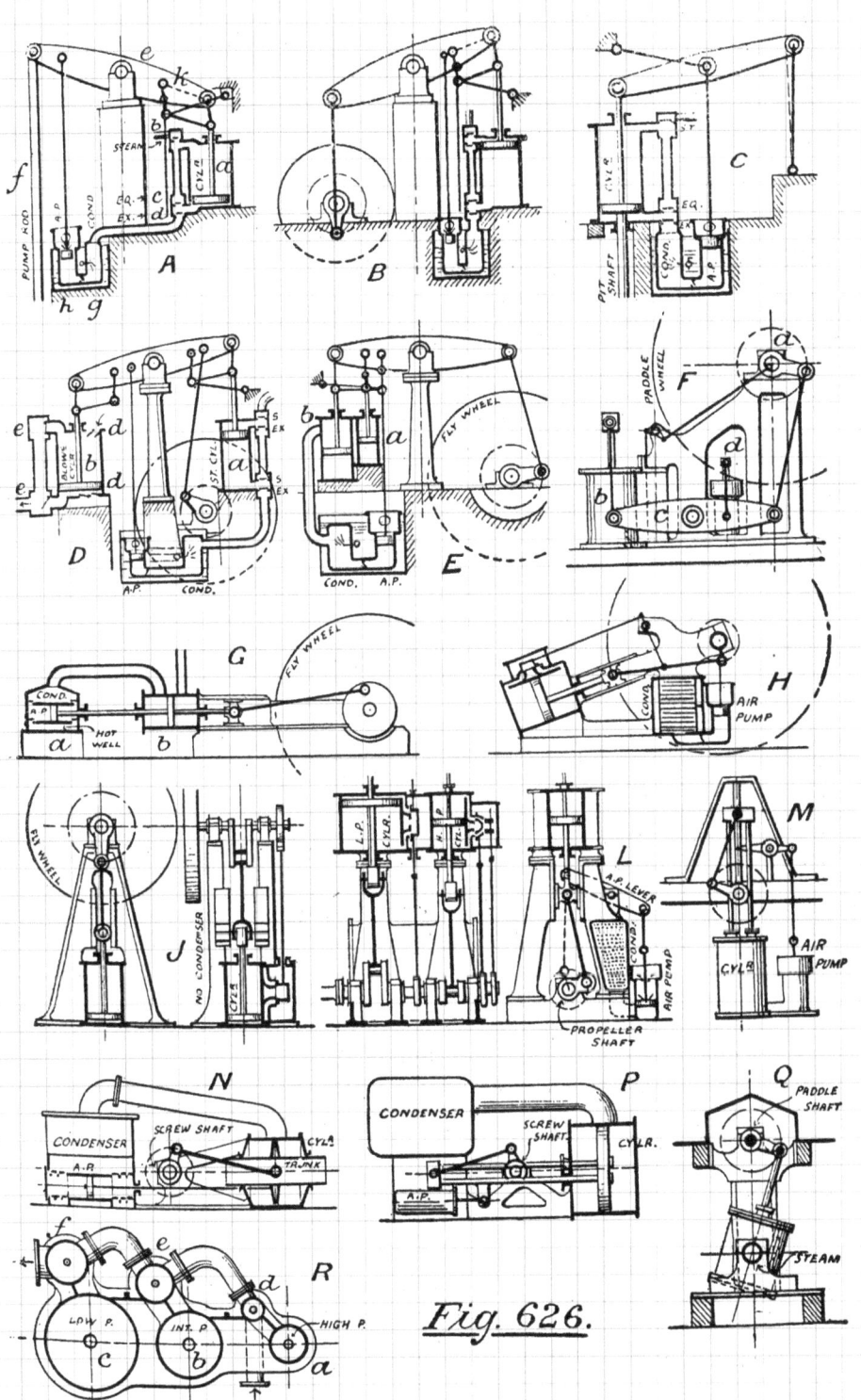

Fig. 626.

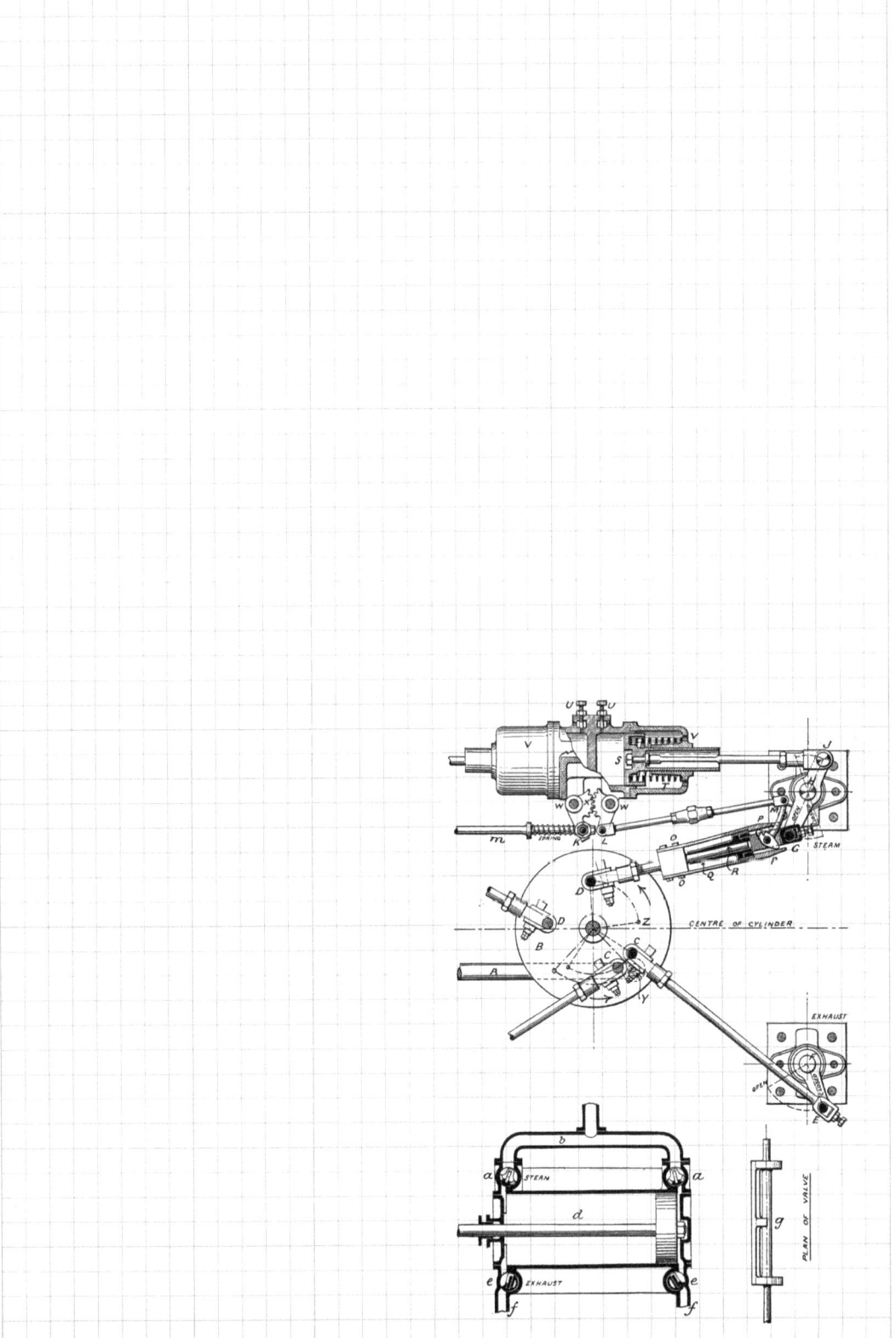

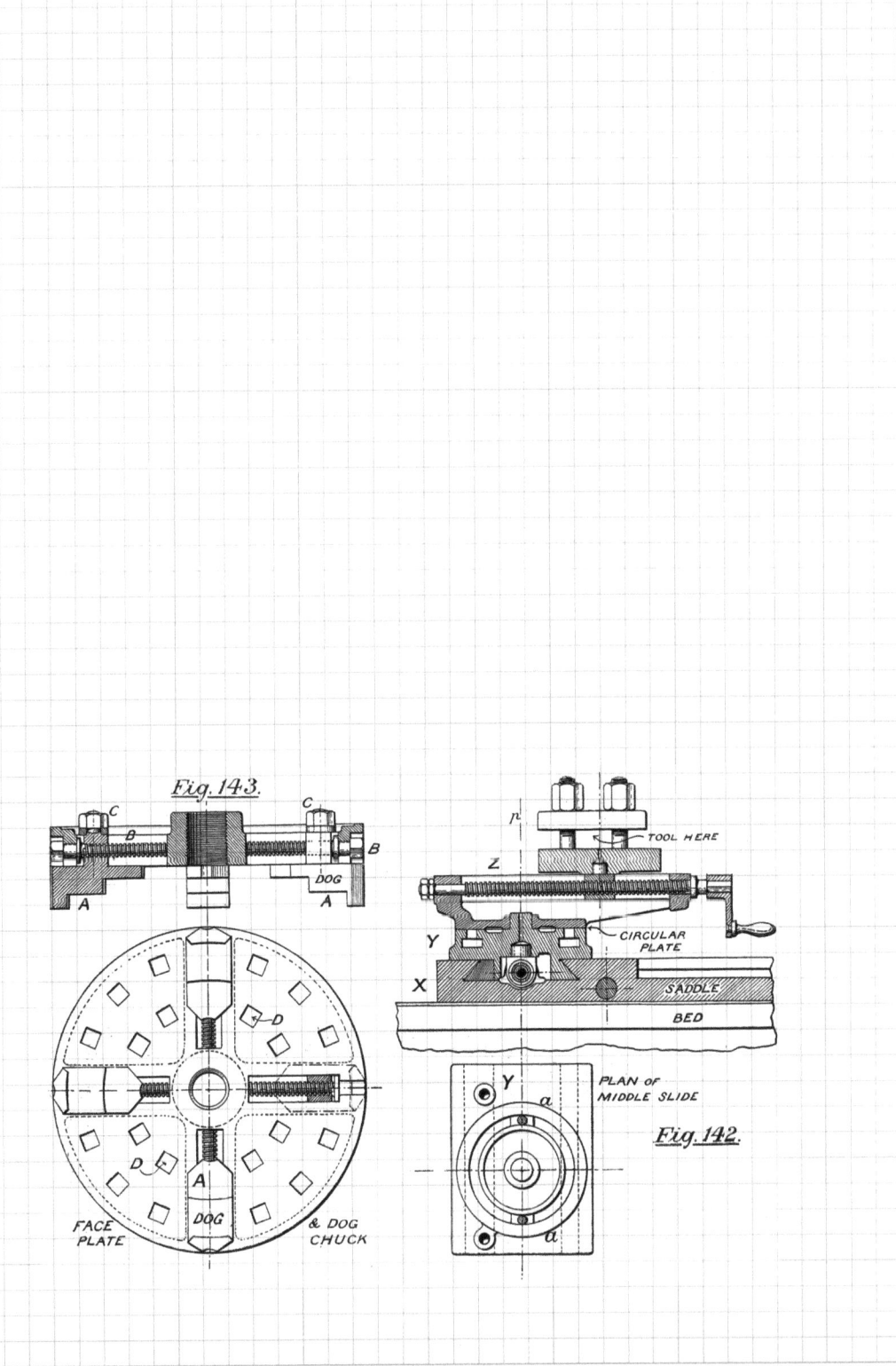

Fig.143.

C
B
A
DOG
C
B
A

FACE
PLATE

DOG

& DOG
CHUCK

D

D
A

TOOL HERE
Z
Y
X
CIRCULAR
PLATE
SADDLE
BED

PLAN of
MIDDLE SLIDE

Y
a

a

Fig.142.

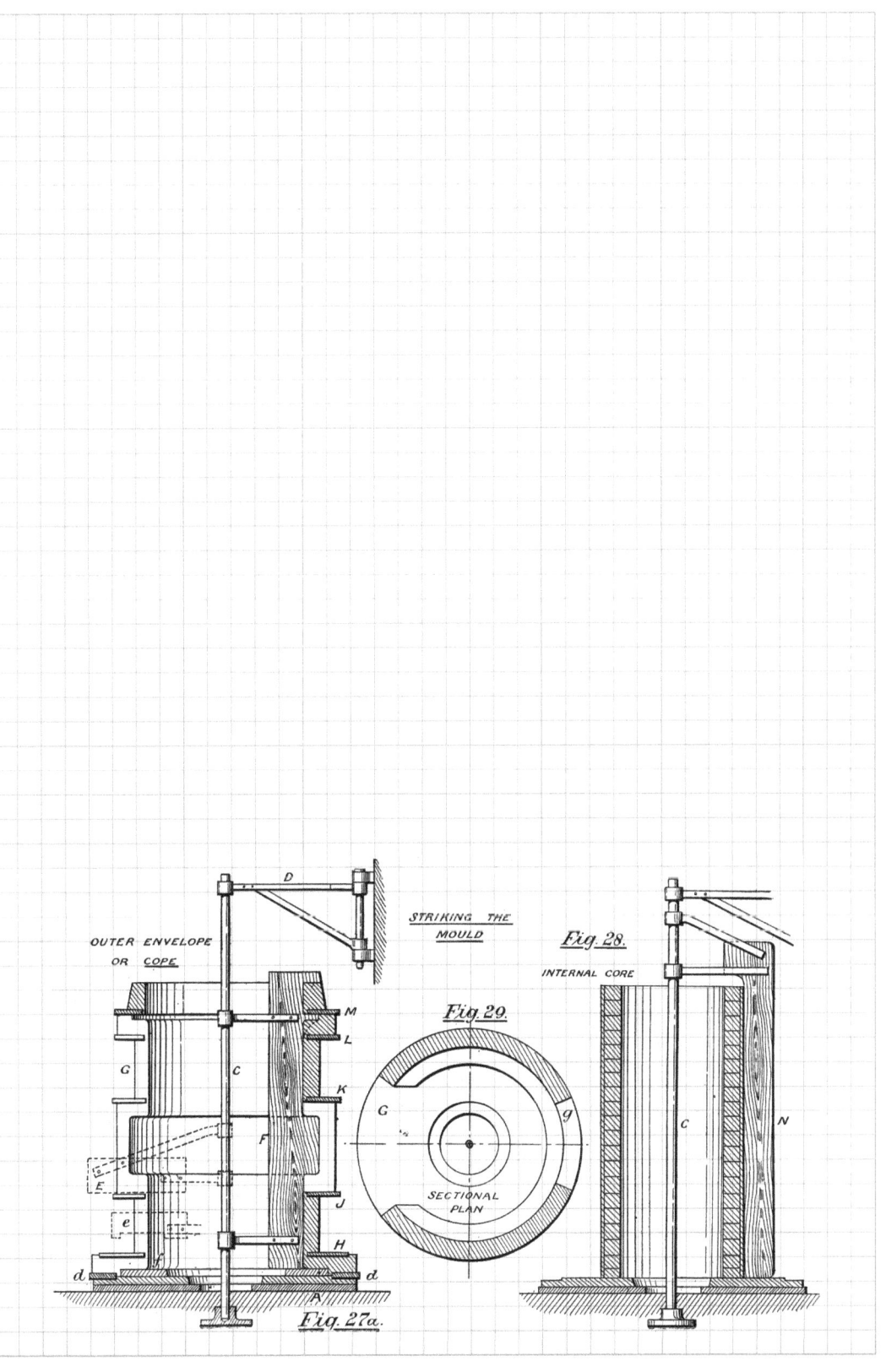

OUTER ENVELOPE
OR COPE

STRIKING THE
MOULD

Fig. 28.

INTERNAL CORE

Fig. 29.

SECTIONAL
PLAN

Fig. 27a.

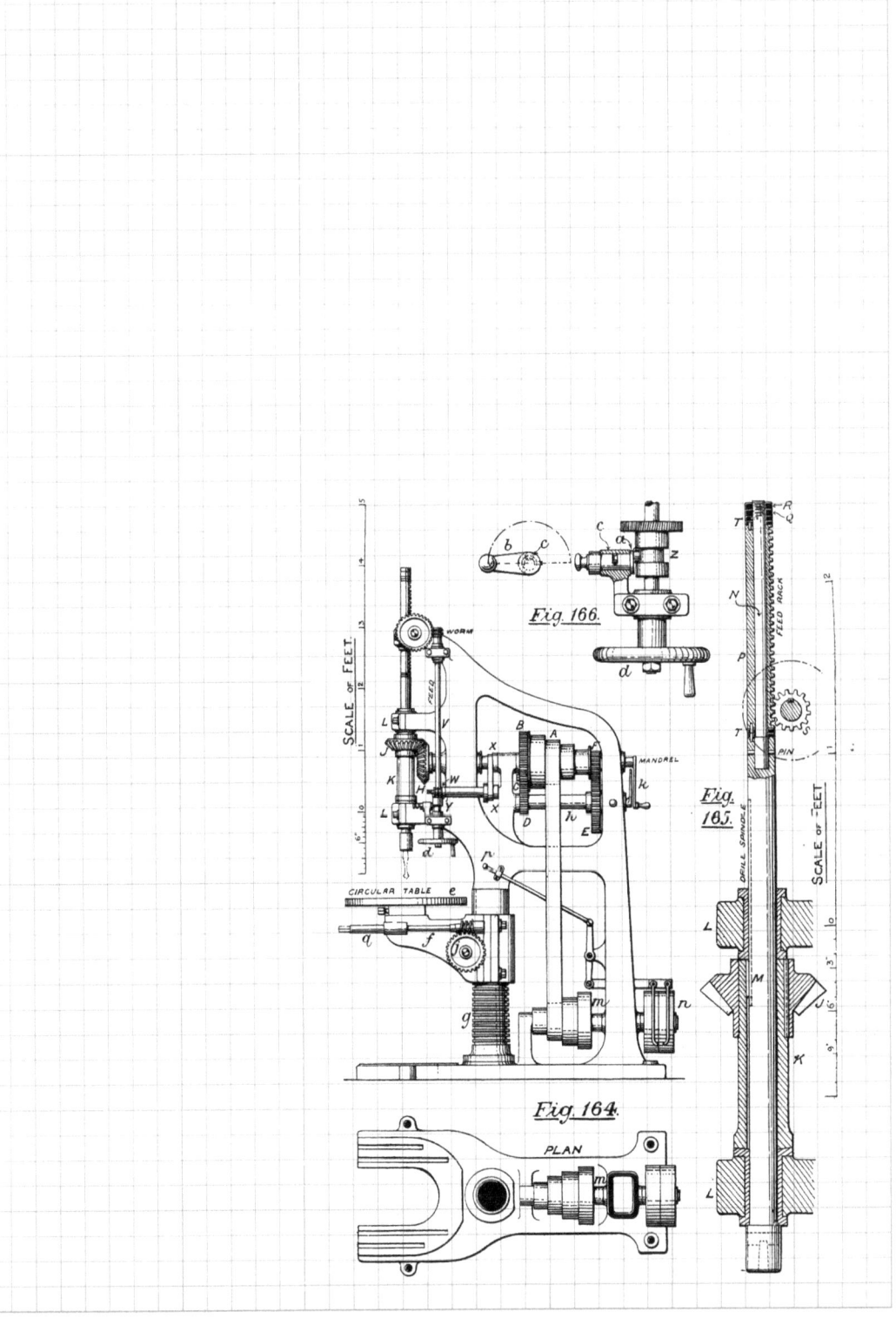

SCALE OF FEET.

Fig. 166.

WORM

FEED

B A

X

X

MANDREL

k

c

D

h

E

CIRCULAR TABLE e

q

f

g

m

n

Fig. 164.

PLAN

m

Fig. 165.

T R Q

N

FEED RACK

P

T

PIN

DRILL SPINDLE

SCALE OF FEET

L

M

K

L

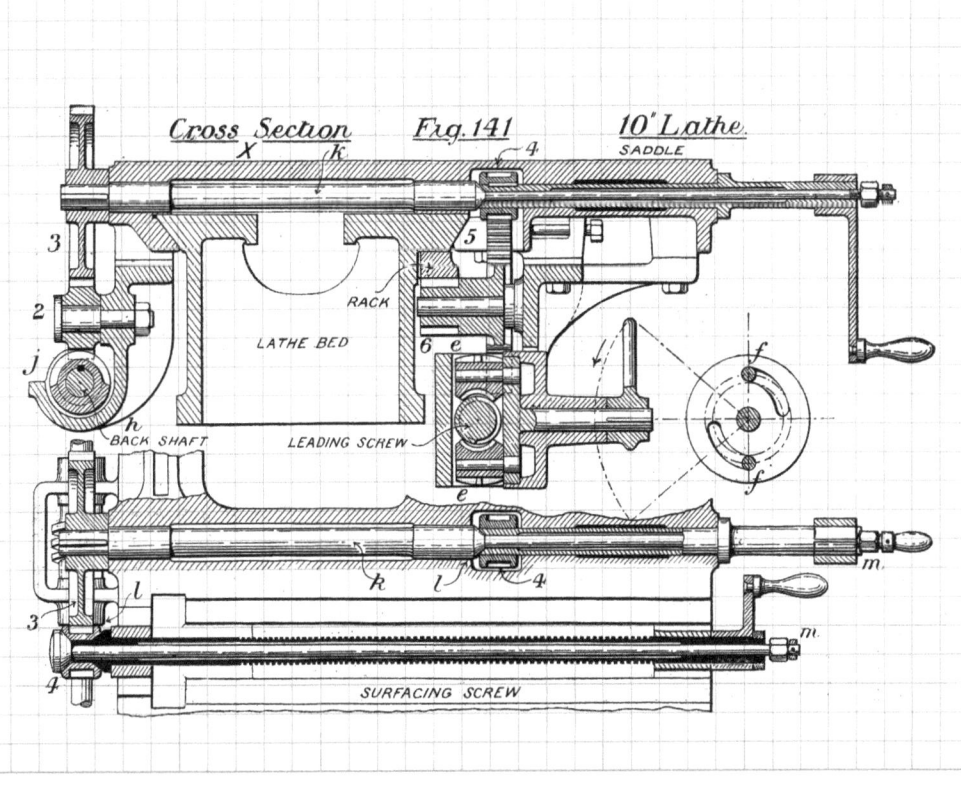

Cross Section   Fig. 141   10" Lathe

X   k   4   SADDLE

3

2   5

RACK

j   LATHE BED   6   e   f

h

BACK SHAFT   LEADING SCREW

e

k   l   4   m

l

3

4   m

SURFACING SCREW

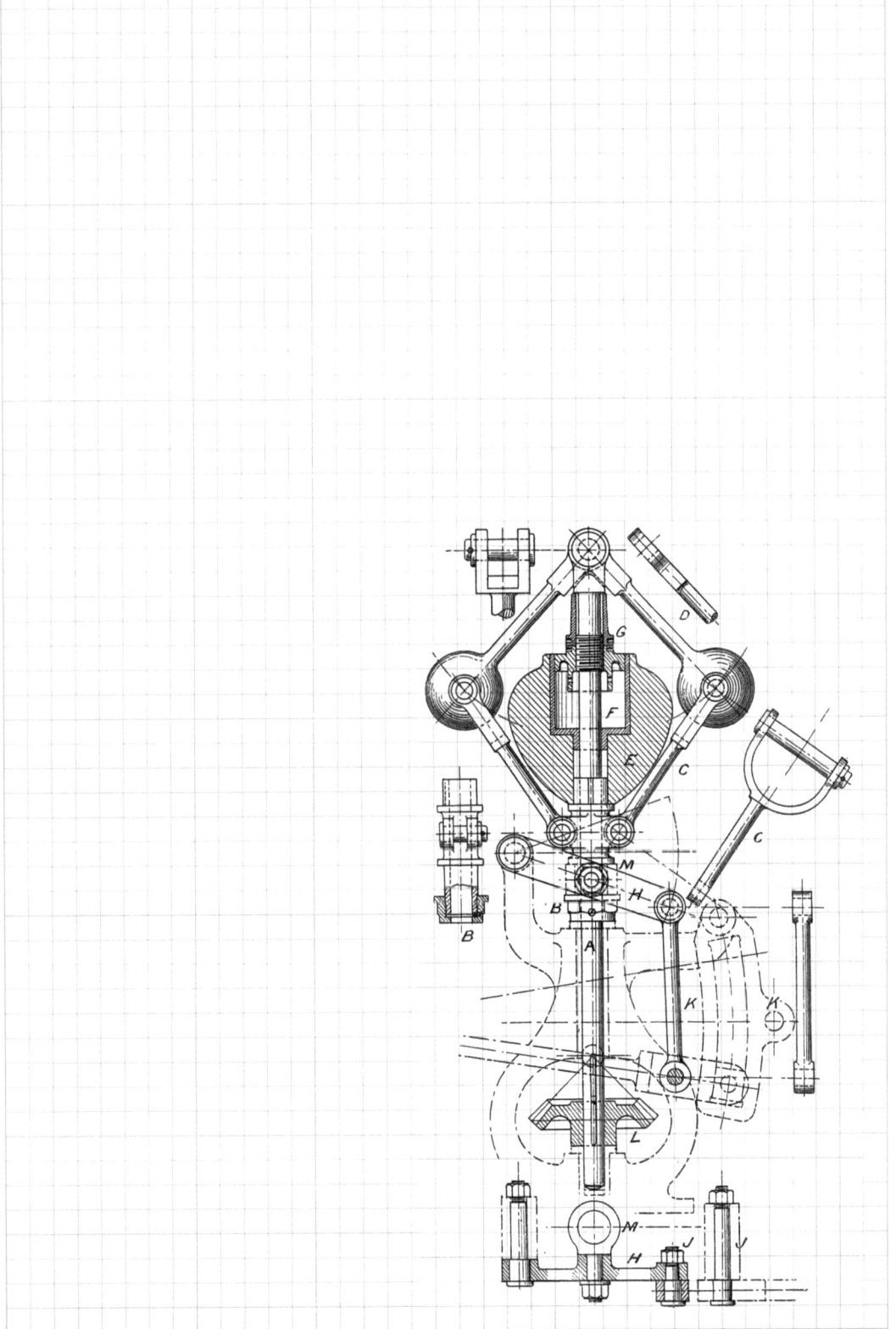

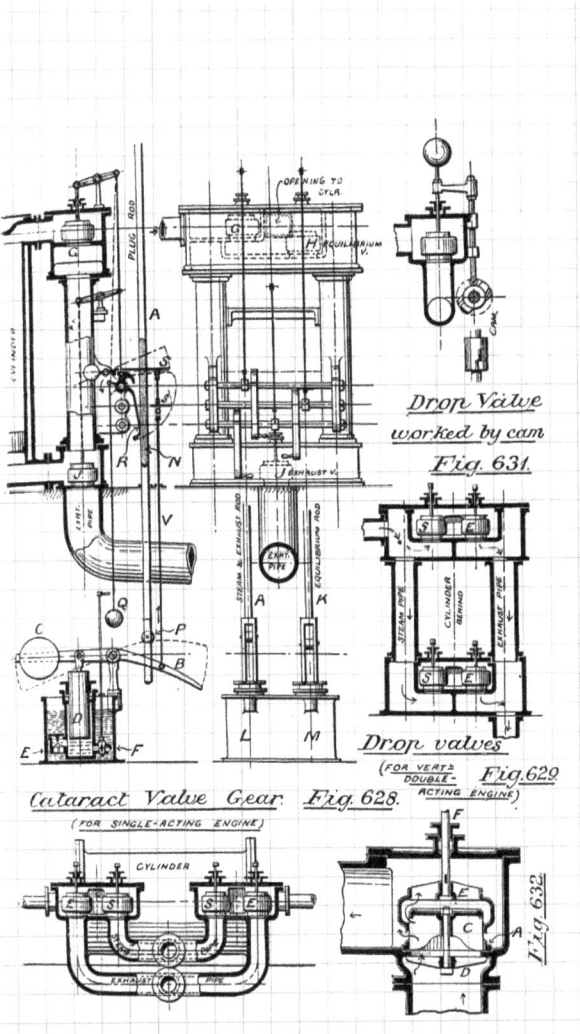

OPENING TO CYLR.

G H EQUILIBRIUM V.

PLUG ROD

CAM.

Drop Valve
worked by cam
Fig. 631.

A

J EXHAUST V.

R N

J

STEAM & EXHAUST ROD

EQUILIBRIUM ROD

EXHT PIPE

V

EXHT PIPE

A K

C

Q

P

B

L M

D

E F

STEAM PIPE

CYLINDER BEHIND

EXHAUST PIPE

Drop valves
(FOR VERT⁵.
DOUBLE-
ACTING ENGINE)
Fig. 629.

Cataract Valve Gear. **Fig. 628.**
(FOR SINGLE-ACTING ENGINE)

CYLINDER

EXHAUST PIPE

F

E

C

A

D

Fig. 632.

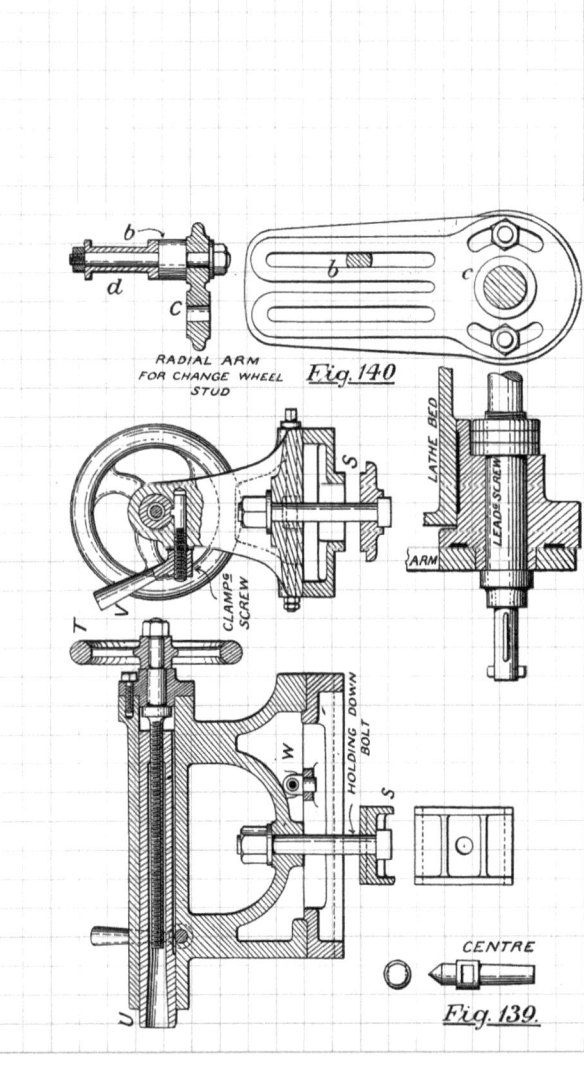

b

d

c

b

c

RADIAL ARM
FOR CHANGE WHEEL
STUD

Fig. 140

S

LATHE BED

LEAD SCREW

CLAMPS
SCREW

ARM

T

V

W

HOLDING DOWN
BOLT

S

U

CENTRE

Fig. 139.

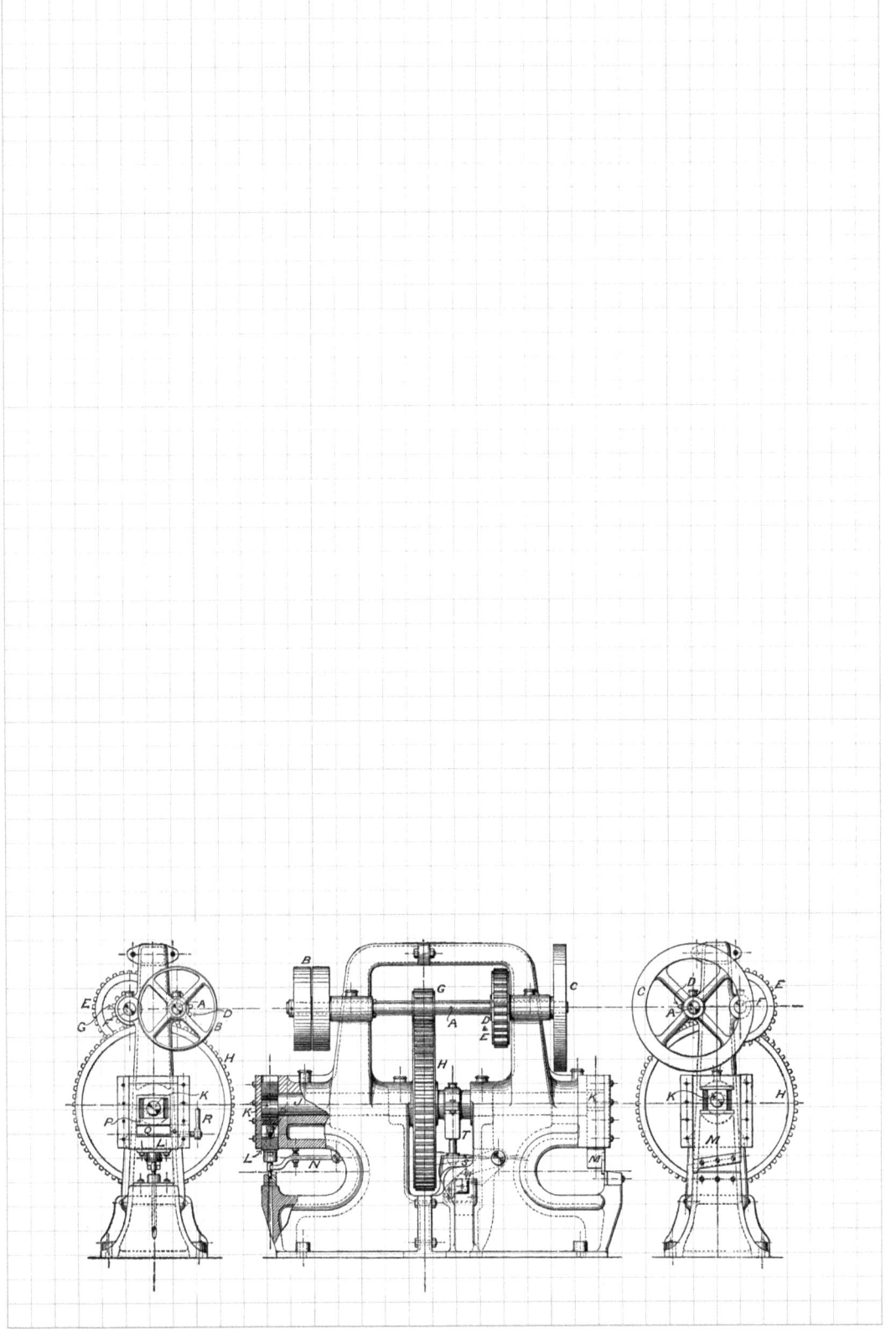

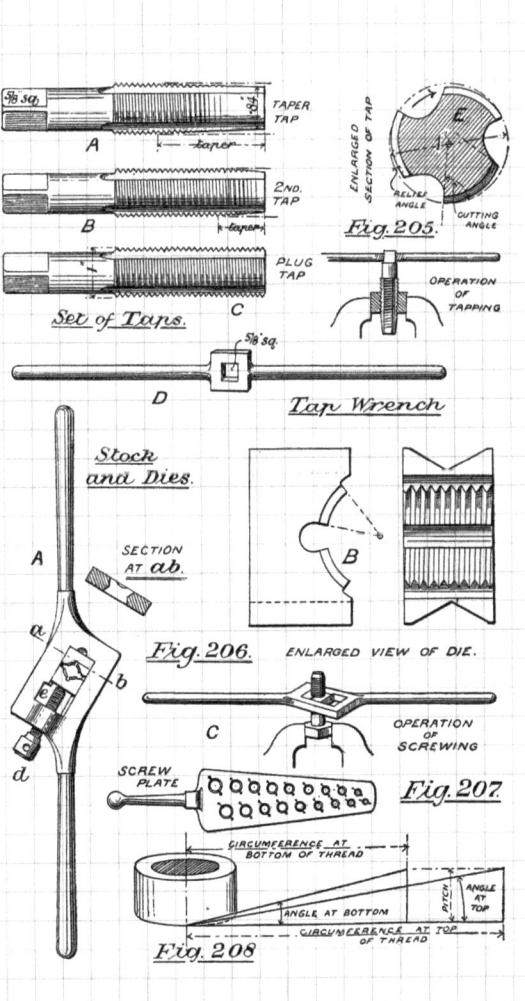

$\frac{5}{16}$ sq.

TAPER TAP

A

taper

Set of Taps.

2ND. TAP

B

taper

PLUG TAP

C

ENLARGED SECTION OF TAP

E

RELIEF ANGLE

CUTTING ANGLE

Fig. 205.

OPERATION OF TAPPING

$\frac{5}{8}$ sq.

D

Tap Wrench

Stock and Dies.

A

SECTION AT *ab.*

a

b

c

d

Fig. 206.

B

ENLARGED VIEW OF DIE.

C

OPERATION OF SCREWING

Fig. 207.

SCREW PLATE

CIRCUMFERENCE AT BOTTOM OF THREAD

ANGLE AT BOTTOM

ANGLE AT TOP

PITCH

CIRCUMFERENCE AT TOP OF THREAD

Fig. 208.

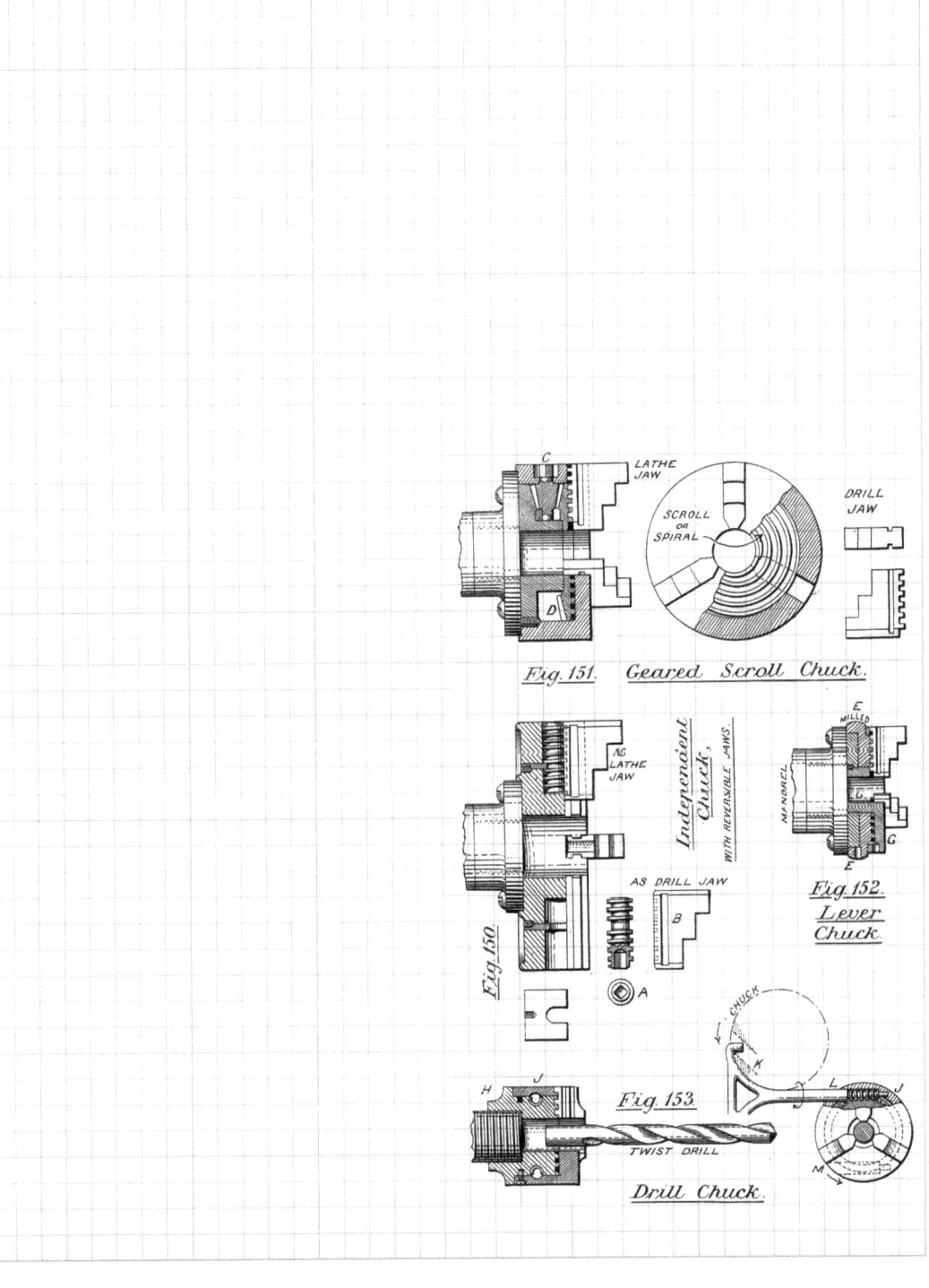

LATHE JAW

DRILL JAW

SCROLL OR SPIRAL

Fig. 151. Geared Scroll Chuck.

AG LATHE JAW

Independent Chuck, WITH REVERSIBLE JAWS

E MILLED

MANDREL

Fig. 152. Lever Chuck.

AS DRILL JAW

Fig. 150.

CHUCK

Fig. 153.

TWIST DRILL

Drill Chuck.

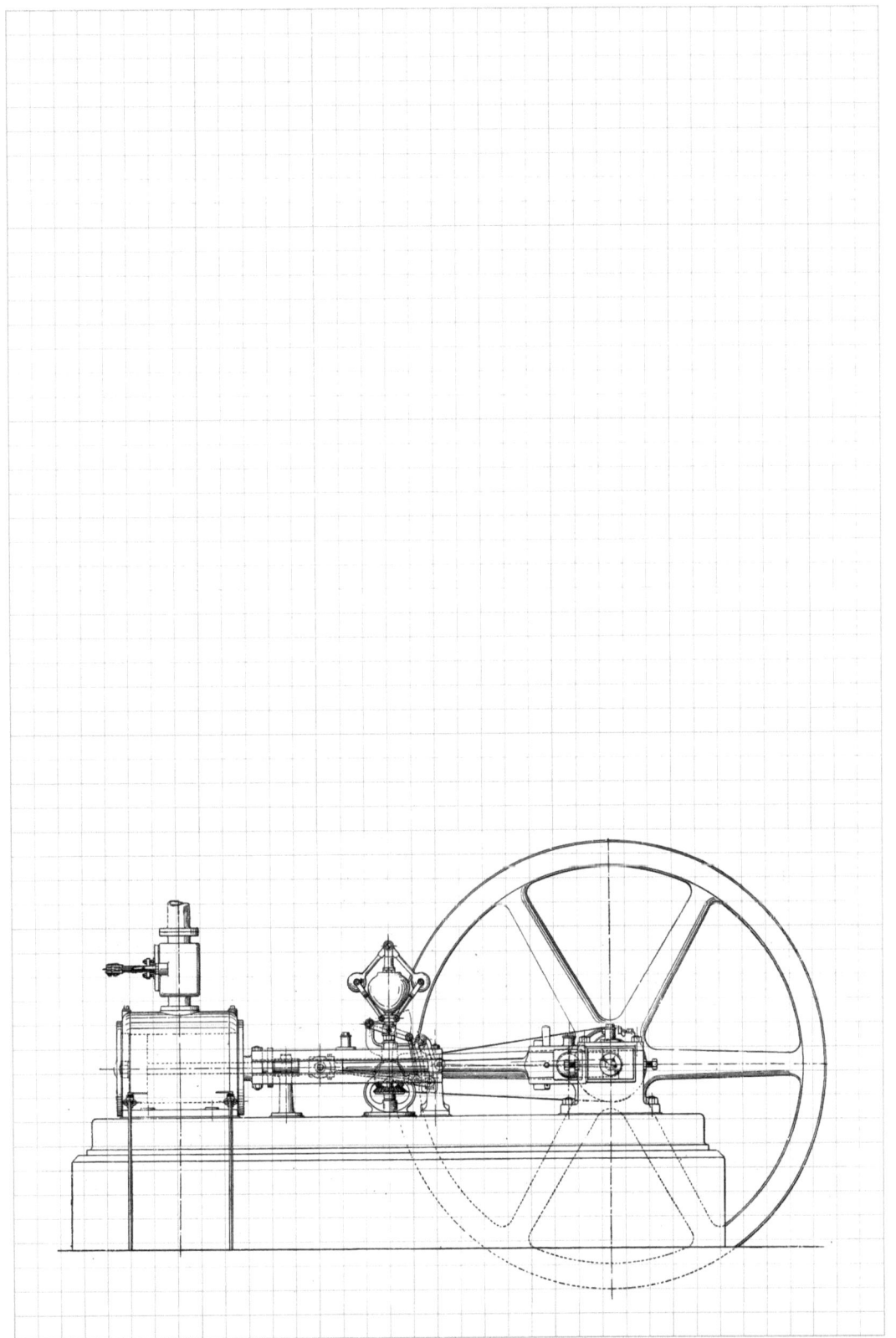

COMPLETE PATTERN

FACE PLATE

BUILDING THE RIM

E

A

B

SHOOTING
BOARD

C

a

a

a

a

FACE PLATE

D

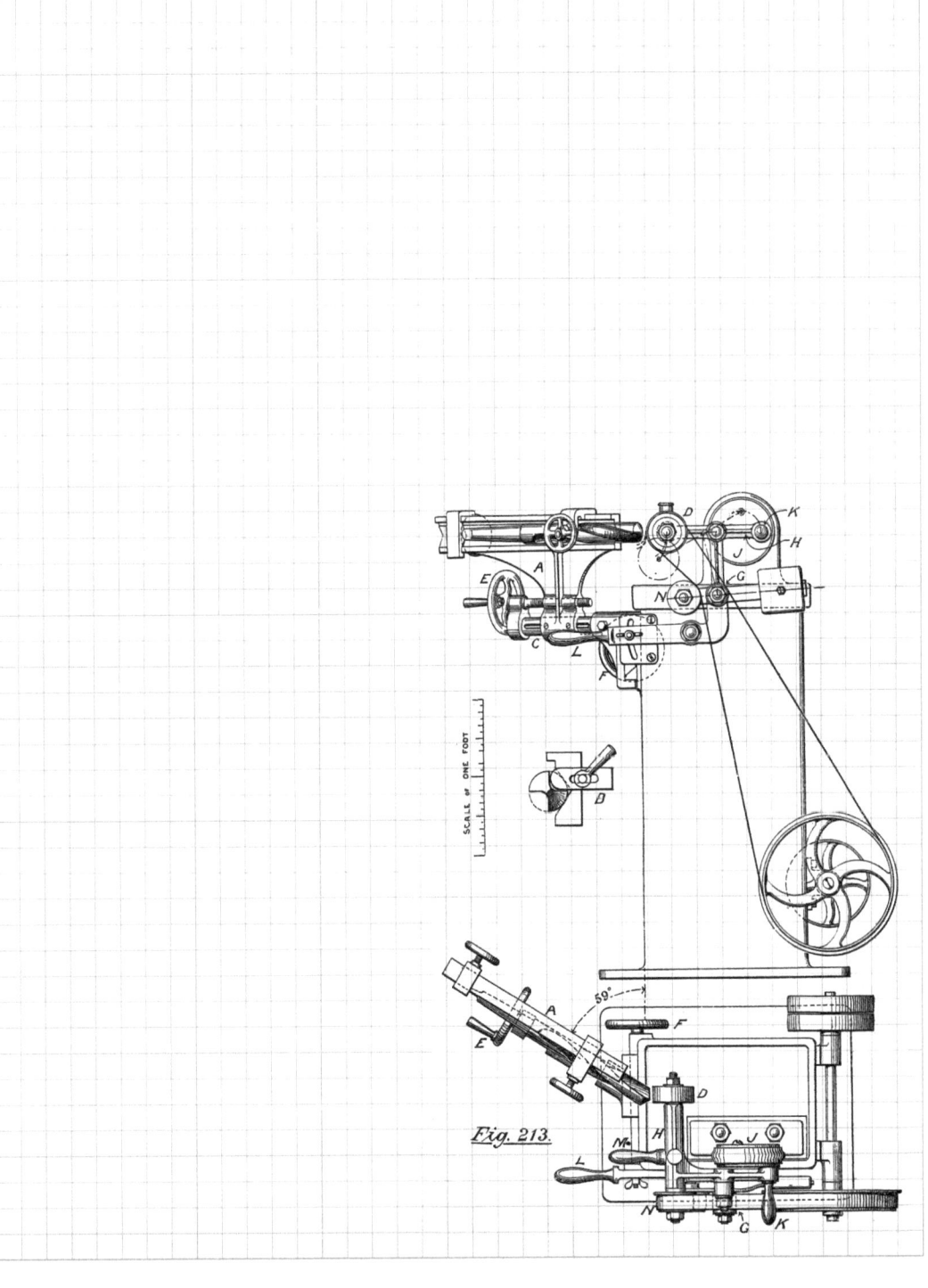

SCALE OF ONE FOOT

Fig. 213.

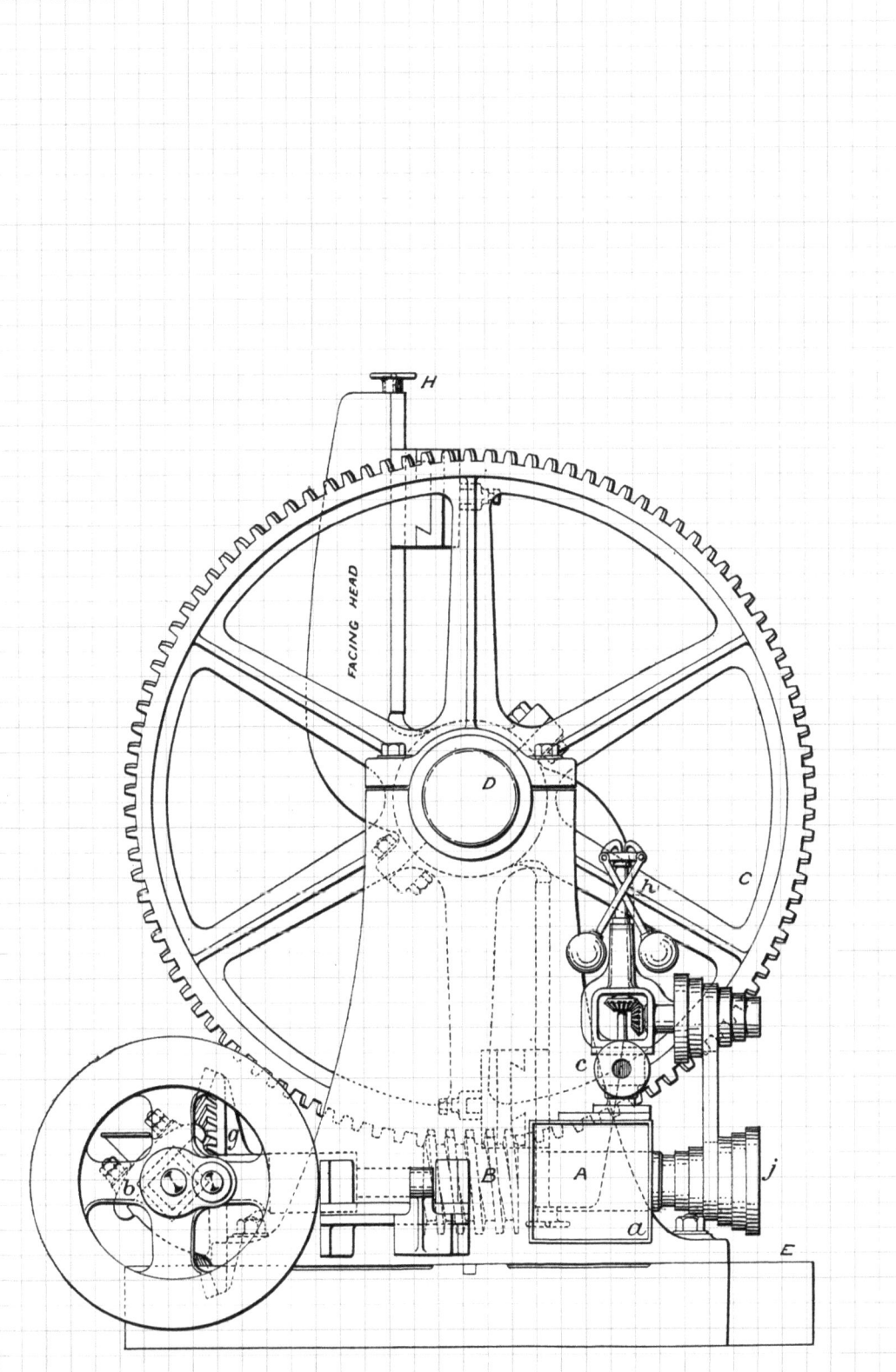

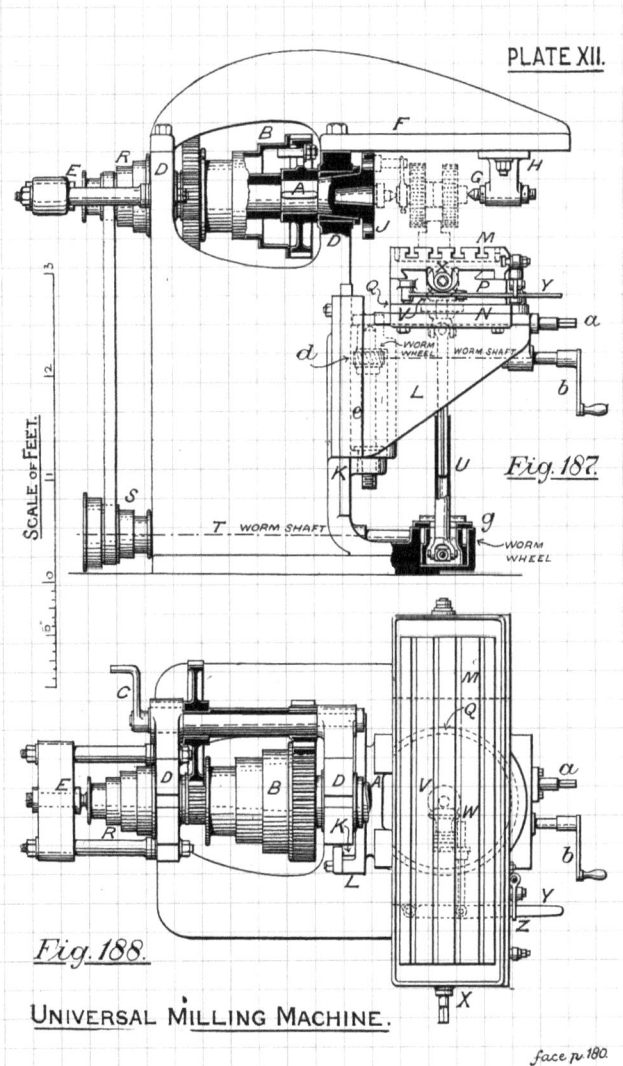

PLATE XII.

Fig. 187.

Scale of Feet.

Fig. 188.

UNIVERSAL MILLING MACHINE.

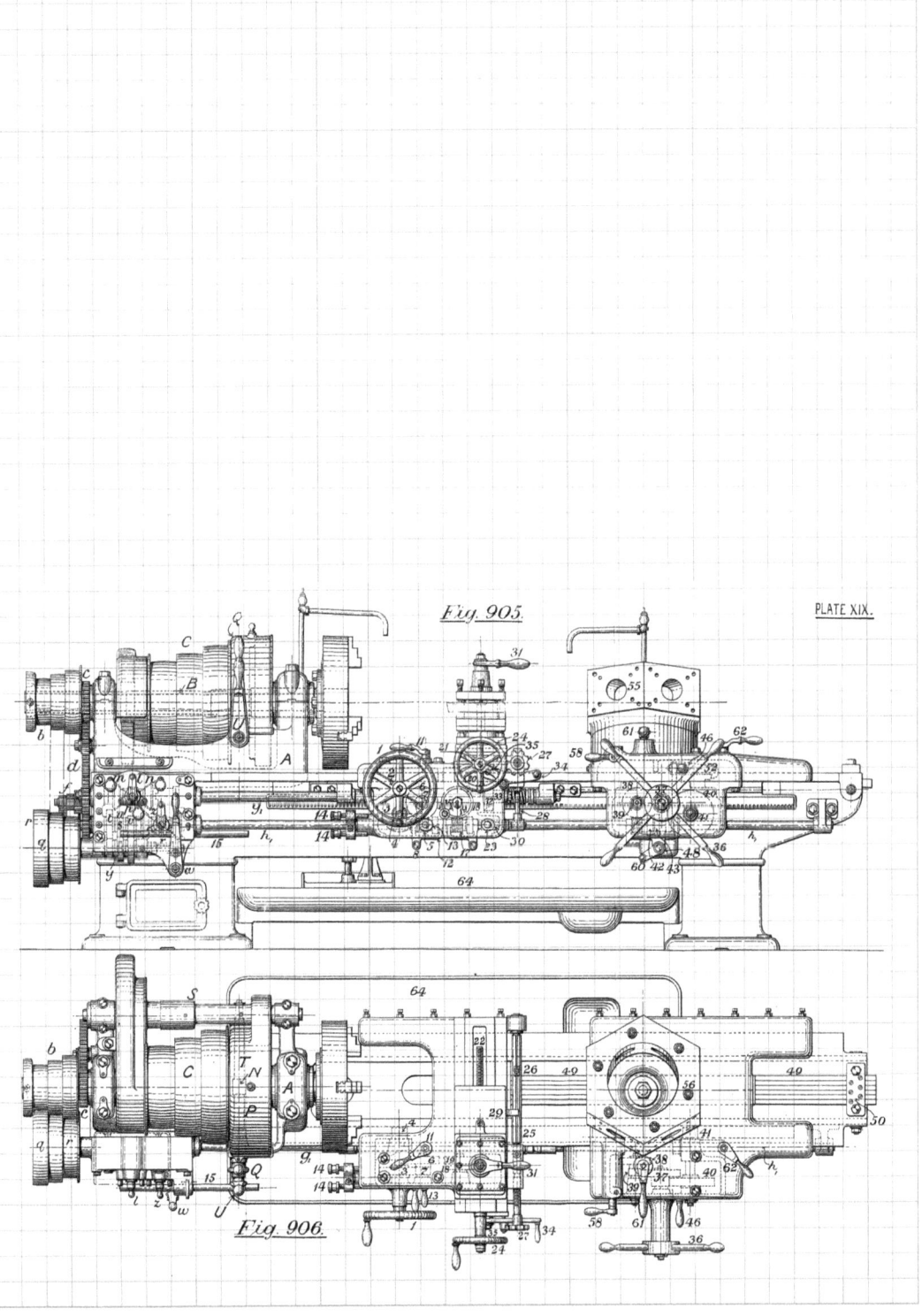

Fig. 905.

PLATE XIX.

Fig. 906.

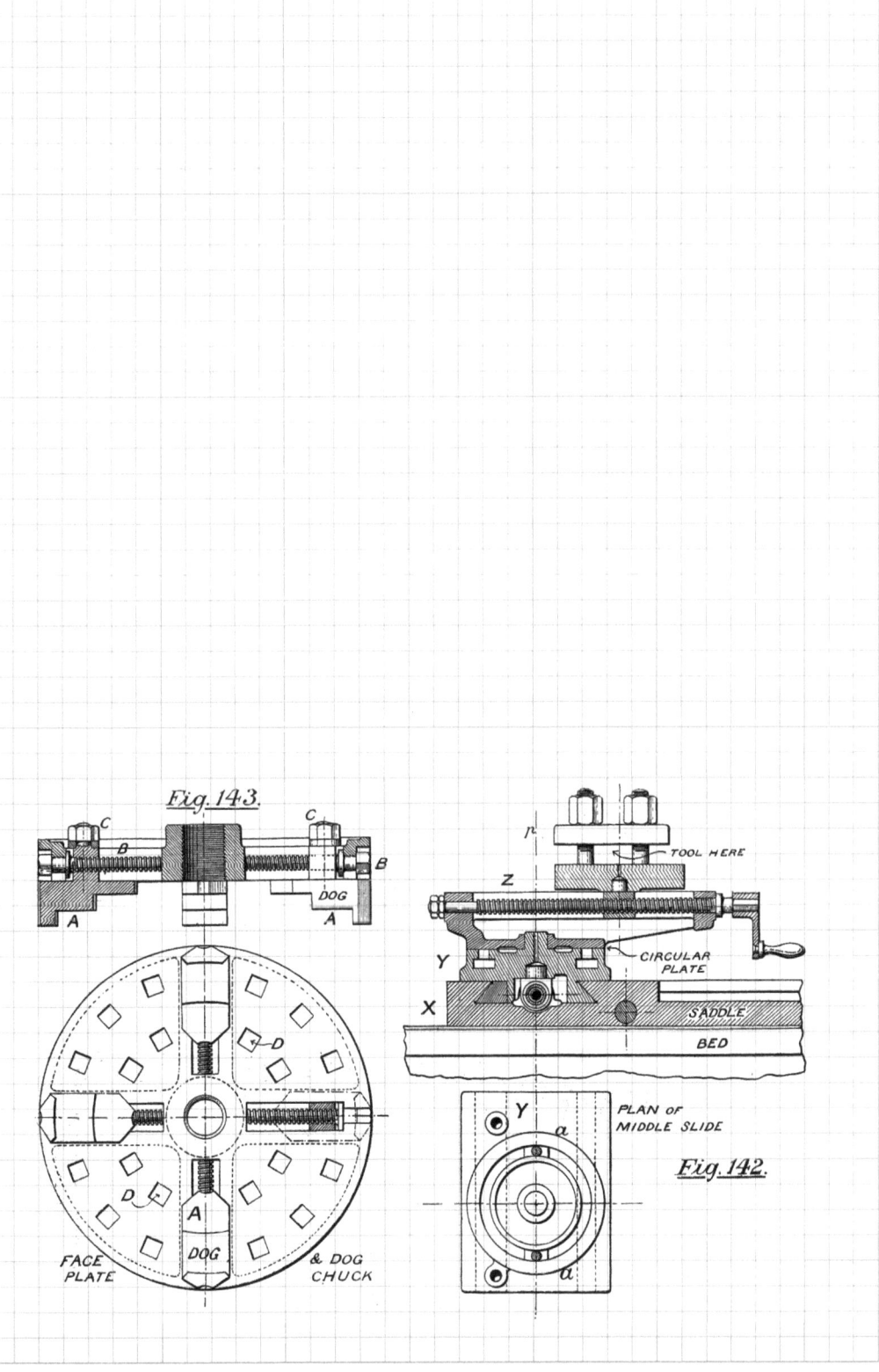

Fig. 143.

C   C
B   B
A   A

DOG

D

D

A

DOG

FACE
PLATE

& DOG
CHUCK

TOOL HERE

Z

Y

X

CIRCULAR
PLATE

SADDLE

BED

Y

a

a

PLAN OF
MIDDLE SLIDE

Fig. 142.

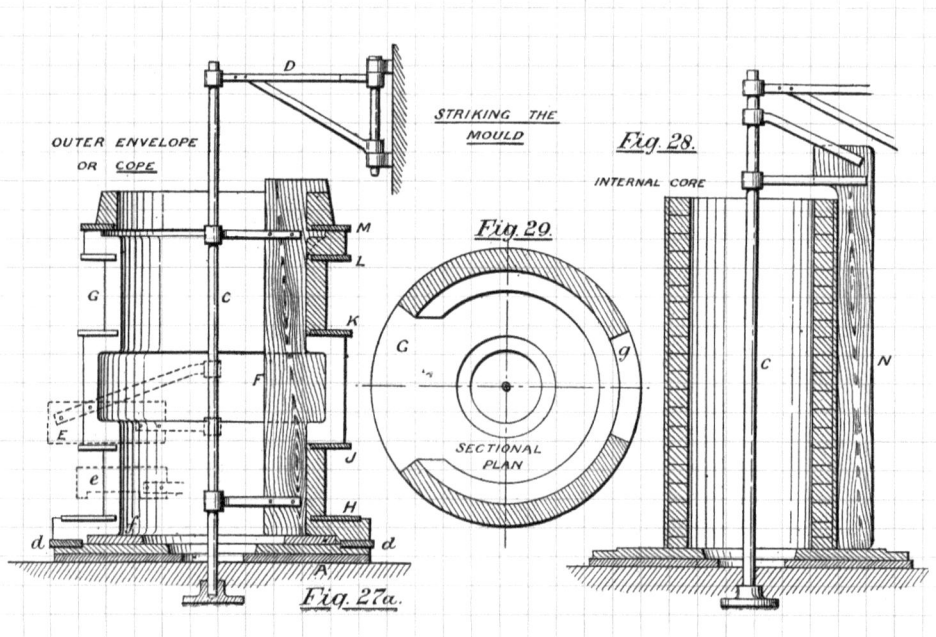

OUTER ENVELOPE
OR COPE

G C

E

e

d d

Fig. 27a.

STRIKING THE
MOULD

Fig 29.

G g

SECTIONAL
PLAN

Fig. 28.

INTERNAL CORE

C N

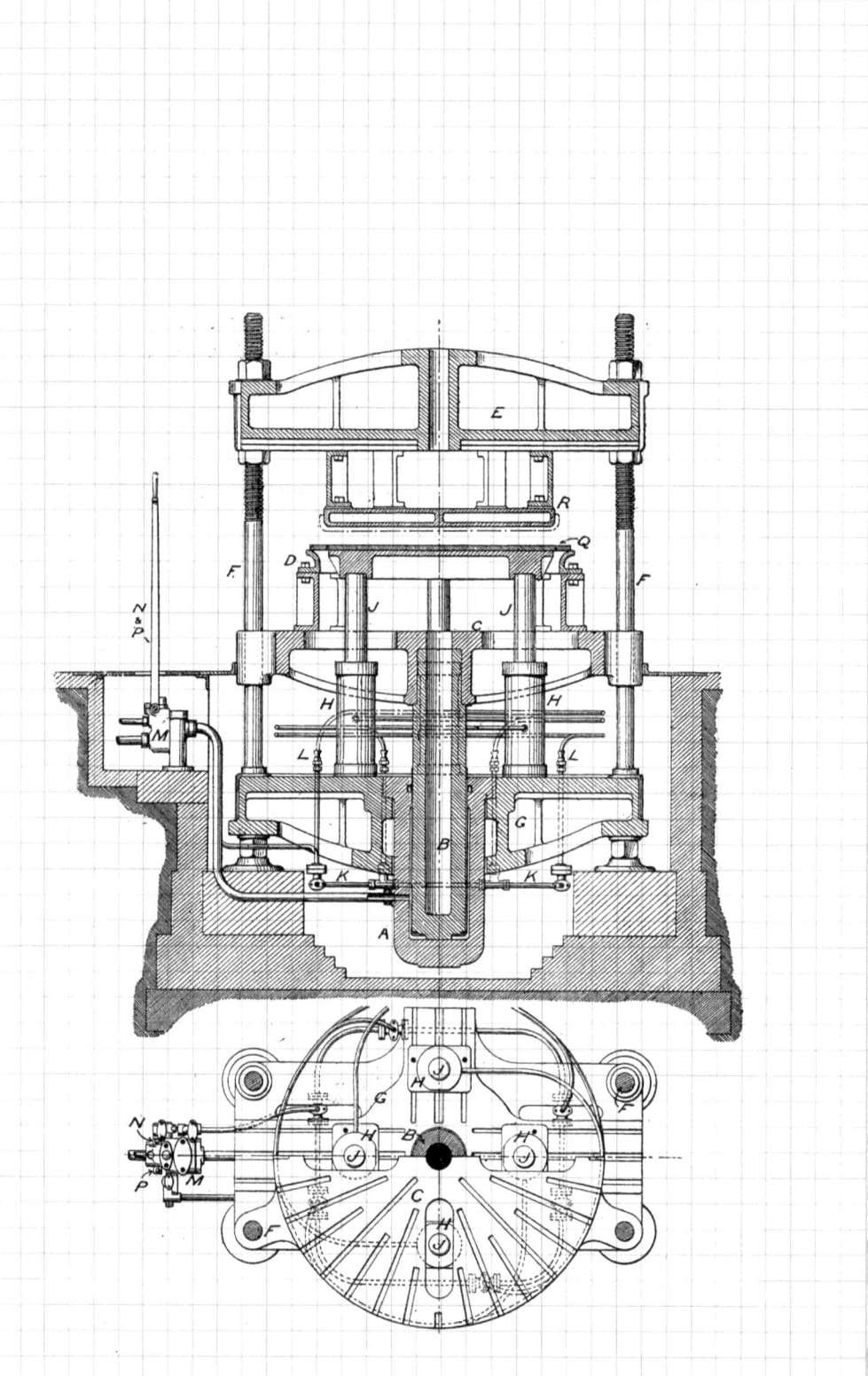

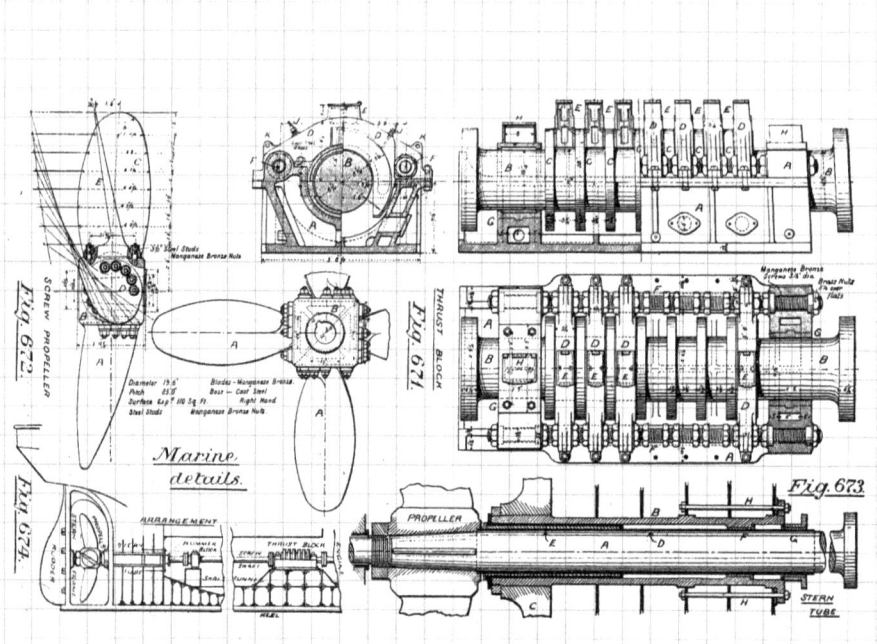

Fig. 672.

SCREW PROPELLER

Diameter 19 6'
Pitch 23 6'
Surface Exp⁴ 100 Sq. Ft.
Steel Studs

Blades - Manganese Bronze
Boss - Cast Steel
Right Hand
Manganese Bronze Nuts

Fig. 671.

THRUST BLOCK

Fig. 673.

STERN TUBE

PROPELLER

Fig. 674.

ARRANGEMENT

Marine.
details.

Alpha Sale Academy

So geht Umsatz

Umsatz kann so einfach sein, das ist das Credo von Steffi Kopf, Inhaberin von Alpha Sale. Die Vertriebsexpertin hat sich darauf spezialisiert, ihren Kunden neue Geschäfts- und Kundenfelder zu zeigen. Sie ist ein passionierter DoorOpener und ausgebuffter Hunter. Zudem machte sie aus ihrem Hobby eine berufliche Passion: Sie bietet für Städte und Hotels Oldtimermarketing als Eventkonzept an.

www.alpha-sale.de

Klassikfreunde Baden

Wir lieben altes Blech

Die Klassikfreunde Baden existieren seit 2019 und wurden von Steffi Kopf ins Leben gerufen. Die Gemeinschaft ist offen für alle Marken historischen Blechs. Steffi Kopf entwickelt, plant und leitet "abgefahrene" Themenausfahrten zu echten Geheimtipps in Baden-Württemberg.

www.klassikfreunde-baden.de